Women in Ministry Today

by
Helen Beard

Distributed by Logos International
Plainfield, New Jersey

All Scripture references are taken from the King James Version, unless otherwise noted TAB (The Amplified Bible) or NIV (The New International Version).

WOMEN IN MINISTRY TODAY
Copyright © 1980 by Helen Beard
All rights reserved
Printed in the United States of America
Library of Congress Catalog Card Number: 80-82388
International Standard Book Number: 0-88270-447-8
Distributed by Logos International, Plainfield, New Jersey

From the Heart of the Author

This teaching of Spirit-filled women in the ministry is presented to you in the hope that you will be set free from the bondages of law into the glorious liberty of Christ. It is impossible to plunge deeper into the power of the death and resurrection of Christ while we are still clinging to the beggarly elements of law.

God wants us to think more in terms of grace and not in terms of law. He wants us to grow in grace from one degree of glory to another as we continue to behold His face.

By the grace of God, I have learned not to be concerned if people do not accept the idea of a woman minister. I have seen that, in spite of the opinions of people, the ministry gift that a woman possesses will make way for itself if that woman is trusting God and not her own efforts and demands. The gift will bear fruit as the primary focus is the liberating power of *agape* love. Death to self will produce life in others.

WOMEN IN MINISTRY TODAY

May we all pass from one degree of glory to another (2 Cor. 3:17-18). We invite you to walk together with us as the bride of Christ.

Contents

Introduction ix

PART ONE:
Spirit-Filled Women in Ministry 1
1 The Promise of Ministry to Women 3
2 The Many-Faceted Ministry of Women 23
3 Women in the Bible and Today 31

PART TWO:
The Governing Principle of All Ministries 41
1 The Way of the Cross 45
2 Neither Male Nor Female in Christ Jesus (Galatians 3:28) 61

PART THREE:
Some Important Bible Terms 79
1 The Meaning of "Headship" *(Kephale)* 83
2 The Meaning of "Submission" *(Hupotasso)* 107
3 Other Terms 115

PART FOUR:
Questions and Answers 127
1 Basic Questions 129
2 Further Questions for Thought and Reflection 141

PART FIVE:
Women in the West Today 156
1 A History of Struggle 157
2 The Little Foxes That Steal the Grapes 167

PART SIX:
Single or Married 174
1 For Singles Only 175
2 The Beautiful Ministry of the Homemaker 191

PART SEVEN:
Our Legal Rights in Christ 228
1 "Now" Power 229
2 A Personal Testimony 235
In Closing: From the Heart of the Author 241

Bibliography 243

Introduction
by Cliff Beard

It was about one o'clock on a summer day in Idaho Falls, Idaho, when an urgent letter arrived from Rev. David Cartledge, a well-known Australian charismatic minister and author of a charismatic magazine called *Contact*. In the letter, Rev. Cartledge requested an article written by Helen, my wife, on the subject of Spirit-filled women in the ministry. It was this request that caused us to pray diligently for the Holy Spirit's guidance, not really expecting the outstanding result that followed.

The anointing of the Holy Spirit fell on Helen that day. Soon she was writing. Papers, books, and concordances were opened and seemed to be sprawled across the desk and floor. God was obviously speaking, and the pen was spelling out His words for thousands of people to read. For hours nonstop, Helen was writing. Two nights went by without Helen having any sleep. I was aware of the glorious presence of the Holy Spirit that filled our home. It was for this reason that I knew better than to speak or break in on the communion between Helen and the word of the Lord that was coming forth.

The purpose of this book is to help many struggling husbands and wives with their families. The truths are revolutionary in some areas. But before you make decisions about the book's teachings, we request that you pray for the guidance of the Holy Spirit.

Because of the scores of people who have been helped by Helen's other books *(Release of the Inner Man* and *Love and You)*, I have been praying daily for this tremendous manuscript to be born. Literally thousands of women and men vexed by all kinds of complexes have requested sound truths on this subject.

Together, we have practiced these truths for twenty-five years. They have become our life and happiness, producing the spiritual blending that every married couple needs in ministering together. Life grows more glorious in the presence of God's love.

It is our humble desire that God will take the words of this book and bless your home, family, and church with it. Pass it on; and, if it has blessed you, please write and tell us what it has done for your life. Write to:

Cliff and Helen Beard
P.O. Box 580   P.O. Box 921
Mildura, Victoria   or Idaho Falls, Idaho 84301
Australia   U.S.A.

We appreciate all who have had a part in this book, particularly our dear friend Rev. Patricia Harrison, who

Introduction

holds all the highest qualifications in the fields of New Testament Greek, Hebrew, church history, New Testament customs, the Roman *Patria Potestas,* and many other fields of biblical background. Pat left no stone unturned in rechecking all biblical information in the editing of this manuscript. We are most thankful for this help.

Women in Ministry Today

PART ONE

Spirit-Filled Women in Ministry

The Right Approach

At the request of many men, women, ministers and Christian magazines, it is our pleasure to share with you gleanings from the Scriptures on Spirit-filled women in ministry. At all times the rules of interpretation have to be applied when searching out truth, and this we will seek to do.

When letters were written to the New Testament churches, the writers were dealing with situations which existed in these particular local churches, or instructing and imparting knowledge to churches. We have all seen too much Scripture taken out of context, people ignoring the existing situation and disregarding the subject being dealt with. Some of our well-known ministries today are doing this very thing.

Truth taken out of context becomes distorted truth, and it is very difficult to discern, even for the learned, for it somehow puts a veil over our hearts and minds. Second

WOMEN IN MINISTRY TODAY

Corinthians 3:6-18 explains perfectly what is happening today: some are still bringing forth the ministration of condemnation through the letter of the Law when it ought to be the ministration of righteousness through the Spirit, by grace. This unhealthy ministry is difficult to discern because the same Scriptures and words are used as in spiritual ministry, but the *spirit* behind their use is wrong. For this reason we have a heavy burden in our hearts that the veil be taken away. Christ has done this at Calvary, yet we need to have it manifested in our lives that we may discern the Spirit of truth.

"May the Holy Spirit supply the grace of God to our hearts" is our prayer, "and may the love *(agape)* of God rule in hearts." This is our earnest desire as we enter into this message.

1
The Promise of Ministry to Women

Prophecy

We shall never forget that day when Peter stood up and spoke these words on the occasion of the great outpouring of the Holy Spirit: "And it shall come to pass in the last days, saith God, I will pour out of my Spirit upon all flesh: and your sons *and your daughters* shall prophesy, and your young men shall see visions, and your old men shall dream dreams: And on my servants *and on my handmaidens* I will pour out in those days of my Spirit; and they shall prophesy" (Acts 2:17-18, emphasis added).

What a glorious day that was for all humanity, when the Holy Spirit, the wonderful third Person of the Godhead, came into us to abide with us forever, enabling us to minister in His power; our heart rejoices and our tongue is glad! Here we see that all saved women (daughters and handmaidens) are included in that ministry; we women will also prophesy. Let us now consider

the word translated "prophesy." Strong's and Young's concordances and Vine's New Testament dictionary give the following meanings:
1. speaking under inspiration (inspirational preaching)
2. publicly expounding (truth unfolded)
3. revealing the will and mind of God
4. flowing forth (in a gift)
5. revealing the counsels and ways of God.

It would appear that the word "prophesy" has many different meanings. Upon a closer look, however, we see that these differences actually complement one another to fully express the meaning of the word "prophesy." God knew what He was doing when He allowed for such a vast range of meaning for this word. This range includes:
1. inspiration by the power of the Holy Spirit
2. preaching God's Word, expounding (an aspect of teaching)
3. revealing God's Word
4. flowing forth in a gift of utterance within the framework of God's Word.

We have all been guilty of narrowing this wonderful ability of prophecy to one particular idea, either to utterances given forth, as a spontaneous gift of the Spirit, or at the other extreme, to simply teaching and preaching God's Word. Let us remember, it includes all these, as one is empowered by the Holy Spirit. This means that women may, by the power of the Holy Spirit:
1. inspirationally preach God's Word
2. inspirationally expound God's Word

The Promise of Ministry to Women

3. inspirationally reveal God's Word
4. inspirationally flow forth, within the framework of God's Word, in a gift.

I have conferred with many of those who have earned the right to speak concerning the Greek meanings of this word. It was generally agreed that the above meanings cover the full scope of the term and that it ought not be narrowed down to any one meaning.

The written Word of God is His will revealed to mankind; it is the very heart of God revealed to this world. It is the revelation of the truth to His Body. Prophecy as a gift of the Spirit can reveal either the message needed by a particular people at a particular time, or it can reveal the one needed by the whole Body at a certain time.

Prophecy can at times reveal the hearts of men and, at other times, reveal things to come. The prophetic gift was given both to men and women, and it is much emphasized in Acts 2 and in 1 Corinthians 14. We ought to know, then, its full meaning and purpose.

The nine gifts of the Holy Spirit mentioned in 1 Corinthians 12 and 14 are for men and women (and children). We should not be guilty of failing to appreciate what was given to us in Acts 2. We should take full advantage of the power of the Holy Spirit's enabling abilities.

Women Ministers or Prophetesses

What a glorious day it was for us when Christ arose from the grave and ascended up on high to be seated on the throne! On that day His Body was born into this world and His people, the Church, began a life never known under the Old Covenant. How our hearts rejoice and are filled with deep appreciation for His full equipping of the saints, by giving them ministry gifts! In His divine, wonderful plan, we see in Ephesians 4:10-13, "He that descended is the same also that ascended up far above all heavens, that he might fill all things. And he gave some, apostles; and some, prophets; and some, evangelists; and some, pastors and teachers; For the perfecting of the saints, for the work of the ministry, for the edifying of the body of Christ."

These gifts were actually *people* chosen by our Lord for a particular ministry. Thus they are referred to as the five ministry gifts, not to be confused with the nine gifts of the Holy Spirit. Not everyone can serve in the ministry of a prophet, for example, but every believer may receive the power of prophecy given in Acts 2 and 1 Corinthians 14.

Let's look more closely at the ministry of the prophet. There is a difference between a *prophet* and *one who prophesies*. All may prophesy, but that does not make them prophets. A prophet has an office, or calling, chosen by the Lord for a particular ministry, but prophecy as a spiritual gift is given to individuals at various times to edify and build up the Body of Christ. It is very needful for us to clarify this.

Young's, Strong's, Vine's New Testament dictionary, and other Greek concordances and commentaries define a prophet as:

The Promise of Ministry to Women

1. a seer (one who sees spiritually)
2. a public expounder
3. a proclaimer of divine message
4. an inspired speaker
5. a minister
6. an office
7. a supernaturally illuminated expounder and preacher.

This ministry gift is second to the apostle in its authority in the Body of Christ. The prophet has a revelation ministry in God's Word. A prophet gives vision to local churches or to the Body of Christ as a whole, revealing the will and purpose and mind of God. There is a governmental responsibility in this ministry. It is a ministry of authority, and many examples are found in the book of Acts of prophets who worked along with Paul (who was an apostle).

Now, let us see what the Bible tells us concerning women prophets in the New Testament. "And there was one Anna, a prophetess. . ." (Luke 2:36). She served God in fastings and prayers night and day (verse 37). She spoke of Christ and the great redemption promised to all who were looking for this redemption at that time (verse 38). Then in Acts 21:8-9 we find reference to "Philip the evangelist. . . . And the same man had four daughters, virgins, which did prophesy." The reference here is to the ministry of a prophet as in Ephesians 4:11, not to the more widespread Holy Spirit's gift of prophecy, as found in Acts 2 and 1 Corinthians 14. Most commentators agree on this interpretation. The mention of Philip's daughters prophesying would be unnecessary if the passage referred only to the gift of the Holy Spirit, for that is a gift all the Body of Christ had freely been given (1 Cor. 14:1, 31). (The fact that the same passage mentions God sending another prophet to give Paul a particular message tells us nothing concerning the daughters' gifts. God often works through more than one gifted person to accomplish His purposes.)

Now let us look at what the Greek dictionaries tell us concerning women prophets. The Greek word for "prophet" is *prophetes,* and the Greek word for "prophetess" is *prophetis,* which is the feminine of *prophetes.* The Greek Bible dictionaries make no distinction between the office and ministry of a male or female prophet. A prophetess is:
1. a female preacher
2. a female expounder
3. a female minister
4. an office
5. an inspired speaker
6. a seer (one who sees spiritually)
7. a supernaturally illuminated expounder and preacher.

Prophetesses were mentioned in the Old Testament. Deborah was a prophetess (Judg. 4:4). She had a husband, yet he was not chosen. She was the spiritual leader of the Church of that day (Israel). There must have been thousands upon thousands of men belonging to the Church of that day; today Deborah would be judged by some as being proud and neglectful of her role as a

The Promise of Ministry to Women

woman. God's ways, however, are not our ways. He chooses whom He pleases regardless of what we believe. Such callings as these are not for everyone. The ministry gifts of both men and women in the New Testament, as well as the ministries of prophets or prophetesses in the Old Testament, are really made up of a minority of the whole of God's people. In Exodus 15:20 we read that Miriam was a prophetess. Her prophetic ministry differed from that of Deborah. Miriam had a prophetic ministry of praise and worship among the women particularly. Shallum's wife, Huldah, was a prophetess (2 Kings 22:14; 2 Chron. 34:22).

Other prophetesses referred to are Noadiah in Nehemiah 6:14 and a woman in Isaiah 8:3. All prophets and prophetesses have ministries differing one from another; the Lord has not made two alike. He is a Lord of great variety.

What about these ministries in our present day? Charismatic Christians believe that whatever gifts and ministries were enjoyed in the early Church still exist today, even if we do not always recognize them because of our lack of teaching.

There are still prophets and prophetesses in our day who are not known in those terms. Using our present terms—minister, preachers, evangelists, pastors, teachers—we can only define the particular ministry gift by the fruit it produces. All the five ministry gifts can be found in both men and women in our day just as in the New Testament and Old Testament. These are all recognized by the particular fruit the ministry produces.

WOMEN IN MINISTRY TODAY

(The fruit of the particular ministry is proof of the operation of a ministry gift.)

There are usually more men than women exercising ministry gifts; that is the way the Lord seems to have arranged it, probably because many women have home responsibilities. But even so, there still are more women's ministries than we have realized, not only in the United States, but in every country of the world.

Carnal (Sense-ruled, Fleshly) Women in the Local Church

We have looked at the Word of God concerning women's ministries, noticing relevant Scriptures in their context. Thus far we can see plainly in the Word that God has ordained ministries for Spirit-filled women. Now we have a portion of Scripture to deal with which at first glance would seem to contradict what we have said so far. In reality, there is no contradiction.

Read 1 Timothy, chapter 2. Note that Paul is giving instruction to Timothy. He is preparing Timothy to deal with any signs of carnality that might appear in the churches. Paul had already dealt with his same carnality in 1 Corinthians; now he instructs Timothy how to avoid such a situation. Let us note that:

1. Paul is not speaking here about spiritual women.
2. He is not speaking about women's ministries as such.
3. He *is* speaking on the subject of *carnal* women in the Church.

It is important to understand the subject Paul is dealing with. If we understand Paul's subject, then we will understand that everything said is referring to that

The Promise of Ministry to Women

subject and not another. A misunderstanding of the circumstances and subjects confuses many; we must read Scripture in its historical as well as in its grammatical context. Verse 8 of 1 Timothy 2 reads, "I will therefore that men pray everywhere, lifting up holy hands, without wrath and doubting [disputes]." Paul had had this trouble at Corinth; they had been involved in disputes, even over the topics for prayer, and had held hatred in their hearts towards each other.

Verse 9 says, "In like manner also, that women adorn themselves [to put in order] in modest apparel [dress], with shamefacedness [respect—this does *not* mean "shame"] and sobriety [temperance]; not with broided hair [fancy hair styles], or gold, or pearls, or costly array [extravagance]."

Now the Romans had certain customs. Roman law gave enormous power to men. A man had power even to take the life of his wife or daughter if he chose to do so. This was known as the law of *Patria Potestas*. Their law had no respect for women at all. Even if a woman committed a crime, the husband was brought to court!

Prostitutes were known for their elaborate hair styles and overdressing. They wore much jewelry and were bold and brazen in their speech. They stood out in the marketplaces, speaking out with argumentative voices in public to the crowds that went by, trying to entice the men. These manners were their identifying marks. How different it is today; the prostitutes often dress and act more like other women. One does not always know who they are, as they are subtle and deceiving. We do not have the dreadful Roman law hovering over our heads today. But the Christian women of Corinth had the Roman customs of that day deal with. There were carnal Christian women who sometimes dressed and acted in a way which could have made them look like the prostitutes of the day. Needless to say, this was a very bad witness for Christ. They could be mistaken for prostitutes by those who were not Christians. So Paul corrected this, entreating them to act in a way which would give a good testimony to those outside.

Now in the custom of that day, the order of service in meetings was different also. The men sat on one side of the room and the women on the other side (we can still see this today in Eastern countries). Only the men were allowed the privilege of open discussion, according to custom. Women could expound or inspire or speak forth the word of the Lord. But they were not permitted to enter into an argumentative discussion or to ask questions about a matter openly. If they did it would certainly suggest the coarse behavior of prostitutes, thus damaging their testimony. Such discussion was reserved for men.

Verses 11 and 12 read, "Let the woman learn in silence with all subjection. But I suffer not a woman to teach, nor to usurp authority over the man, but to be in silence."

Several comments should be made here. First, the Authorized Version gives us a poor translation of the Greek. *Hesuchia* ought not to be translated "silence." Its meaning is more that of "quietness, stillness, rest, ease," as opposed to movement and loud noise. "Usurp" is not in the original and gives the wrong impression. *Authentein*

The Promise of Ministry to Women

means "to exercise [one's own] authority" or "to lord it over someone else." It often implies an autocratic or tyrannical power. It would hardly have been appropriate in the culture of the times for a woman to lord it over a man in this way. Actually, it would never be right for a man or a woman to exercise his or her own authority—the only authority in teaching is the authority of the Word of God itself.

Whatever one's opinion on the ministry of women, this passage is not as clear, one way or the other, as it might appear. One Greek word means both "woman" and "wife," and another word means both "man" and "husband." So we cannot be certain whether the prohibition is against wives teaching their husbands, or all women teaching all men. Many *assume* it is the latter, but there is no proof that this is the case.

Again, is it meant that: 1) a woman way not teach, and 2) she may not exercise a domineering authority? Or is it meant only that she may not teach in this domineering way, but may do so in a quiet and humble way? We cannot be dogmatic here. Furthermore, there was a recognized teaching office in Paul's day. The teacher, in this sense of the word, sat with his pupils, who were often literally at his feet (just as Paul learned at the feet of Gamaliel). It was common in this kind of teaching situation for heated arguments to develop; occasionally these gave way to violence. Quite clearly it would not look good for a woman to argue with men in public in such a domineering way. The use of *authentein* suggests that very possibly this kind of teaching office is what the apostle is objecting to for women. Other less formal kinds of teaching would not pose the same problems. The important thing was that women behave in a decorous manner and not harm the gospel by their brashness.

The most likely meaning of this text is that women (or perhaps wives) are forbidden to teach *in a particular, domineering and loud-mouthed manner.* If we say this verse prohibits all women from teaching all men, we make the Bible contradict itself, for we have just seen cases of women who did teach men and were approved of God. Both Priscilla and Aquila taught Apollos. The prophetess Huldah in the Old Testament very probably taught in the school of the prophets, where young men were studying. It is rather hard to draw the line between preaching and teaching, and we know for sure that many prophetesses preached ("giving an extended discourse" is one of the meanings of "prophesy," as we have seen).

Some will tell us that women were able to teach only in "private" situations, as in a home, but a little research soon shows there is no biblical support for this idea. In fact there was no such clear distinction between "public" and "private" in the early Church; they met in homes. How many people would have to be present before the meeting was considered "public"? It is easy to see the legalism into which this line of thought would bring us. (It is much like that legalism which says women may only teach other women and children—a claim which has no scriptural backing—and then has to decide at what age boys become men, so that women can no longer teach them in Sunday school!) A prophetic ministry is normally

The Promise of Ministry to Women

very public, anyway!

The other passage often used to minimize women's ministry is 1 Corinthians 14:33-35. This is really no problem at all. Again, this cannot mean that women must be absolutely silent, for in 1 Corinthians 11:5 Paul clearly speaks about women praying and prophesying in church. The discussion of spiritual gifts in the local church also implies that all should use their gifts, not men only. If complete silence were meant, then women could not pray or even sing in church! And the Bible would contradict itself, as well.

Actually, in chapter 14, the men are told to be silent, too, under certain circumstances. He who speaks in tongues should be silent if there is no interpreter present. Also "if anything be revealed to another that sitteth by, let the first hold his peace" (verse 30). Paul's primary concern is *good order* (verse 33, verse 40, and others). Thus there are circumstances under which both men and women are to be quiet. If they wanted to find something out, women were to wait until they got home to ask their husbands (verse 35).

As we have said, in those days the men sat on one side of the building and the women on the other. The women had little education, and so they probably did not always understand what was said. It was natural that sometimes they wanted to ask their husbands, but they disturbed the service by calling out across the room to their menfolk on the other side. *Laleo* (translated "speak" in verse 35) means to "talk, say, chatter, or engage in conversation." It does not mean preach or teach. The word is also used for the chattering and chirping of birds. These women were asked not to chatter or to call out questions.

In the Beginning

In 1 Timothy 2:14-15 we read, "And Adam was not deceived, but the woman being deceived was in transgression. Notwithstanding she shall be saved in childbearing, if they continue in faith and charity and holiness with sobriety." These verses have been quite difficult for the commentators, verse 15 in particular. We can hardly be dogmatic about their meaning. Eve's part in the first sin is mentioned here (in other passages, Adam's sin is stressed). Eve allowed herself to be deceived by the serpent. This does not mean, as some claim, that all women are more easily deceived than men. This is obviously not true.

Many have pointed out that a number of cults were founded and propagated by women (Mary Baker Eddy with Christian Science, Margaret and Katherine Fox with Spiritualism, and so forth). One also has to remember, however, that Mormonism, Jehovah's Witnesses, the Unification Church, Hare Krishna, and many other cults were founded by men. If one is going to argue that because of Christian Science women should come under men's authority, we might as well argue that because of Mormonism men should come under women's authority.

There were some women in the congregations of Paul's day who were deceived, and they were apparently teaching their ideas in a loud, autocratic fashion. This is why Paul had to give explicit instructions to them at that

The Promise of Ministry to Women

time.

To Eve's children were passed on sin and the curse. It would break a mother's heart to be the cause of such a terrible thing. Nevertheless, if they lived godly lives, mothers would be able to win their children to Christ and they would all find redemption. This is one possible meaning of the verse. It may also mean that a good and faithful woman can trust the Lord to bring her safely through the throes and dangers of childbirth. Still others say that the original Greek ("through *the* childbearing") means that Jesus was born of a woman and became her Savior. What is, of course, *not* meant is that there is some new and different way to be saved—by having children!

There may be several layers of meaning here. From what was the woman to be saved? The context suggests she could be saved from the curse. But how shall woman be saved from this curse? Through childbearing. What childbearing? There is only one childbearing which delivered us from the curse in the beginning, and that is the birth of Jesus, which God said would deliver woman and man from the curse (Gen. 3:15). So, Paul goes on to say that through the birth of Christ, woman is delivered from the curse of the Fall and all it entails if a woman continues in faith and love. This faith is both saving and delivering faith, faith in the work done at Calvary; now this can be made real in a woman's life if she walks in the truth of it. Does man still "rule" over woman? Is she still "under" man? No, she now stands back in her original place, by his side, in Christ—if she continues in this faith and love and living for the Lord, in walking in the Spirit.

WOMEN IN MINISTRY TODAY

If woman is delivered from *part* of the curse, she is delivered from *all* of the curse. Christ never did anything by halves. All through history women have been badly treated because of the curse. But, as Christians, we must never do as some try to do and "canonize the curse"—hold it up as something wonderful to preserve for all time! Christ came to deliver us from the curse and to redeem us. Those who continue to put godly women down are in fact working against redemption!

Eve was made to be a "help meet" for man. That means a "helper suitable for him." Some men think this proves the subordination of women—"she is just there to help *me* fulfill *my* ministry." The word used here does *not* mean a subordinate helper. It is mainly used of God himself, the Helper of His people! No one would say that God is subordinate to man's plans! Woman was made to work in a "team," as it were, with man, an equal helper (associate) and a full person in her own right. The Hebrew word *ayzer* (help) occurs forty times in the Old Testament, and never once does it refer to a subordinate helper.

With the curse, woman was put under subjection to the man, but notice how and when. Genesis 3:16 records the curse, not creation. Woman was not originally beneath the man. The fact that she was created after Adam does not prove she was inferior. Nor will woman be inferior to man in glory. Her subordination is temporary only, and is a result of the Fall. Some say that woman was created subordinate and that the Fall just meant her husband would rule over her more harshly. This is not supported

The Promise of Ministry to Women

by the Hebrew. There are several words for "rule," and if this were intended, the Holy Spirit would have selected the word which means "to rule harshly or despotically." The word used is *mashal*. It simply means "to rule." It carries no sense of a special office or ruler and no sense of an oppressive rule. Eve's curse was that whereas before she was *not* ruled over, now she was. Christ is now working for woman's redemption, and a loving husband cooperates with Him in bringing his wife into freedom in Him. We must work *with* the forces of redemption not *against* them! If we wish to canonize the curse, it would also mean we refuse to use weedkillers, labor-saving devices or anesthetics in childbirth, all on the grounds that we must forever accept and submit to the curse as our punishment for sin, despite the fact that Christ has paid the complete price for sin!

Adam and Eve—A Team for Ministry

In the beginning man was alone for a short time before woman arrived, and we are told that man was not complete alone. So God took a rib out of man and made a woman. The word "made" is *panah* in Hebrew, which means "builded, skillfully formed" (not *asah*, the ordinary word for "made"). So woman is the other half of man, as she came out of man. That is why she is called woman, which is *ishah* (in Hebrew), the feminine of ish, man. It literally means "she-man." (Womb-man or female-man, as she came out of him, gives us our English word "woman.")

Now the amazing thing about this is that God gave

woman a mind, intelligence, emotions, a spirit, and body to go with man's mind, intelligence, emotions, spirit, and body. Why was this necessary? So that she could be his helper, a helper suitable to man intellectually, morally, physically, and spiritually.

If this team ministry principle was true for Adam and Eve, then it is true for men and women and sisters and brothers in Christ today. This team ministry was meant to work on every level, in the governmental aspect of the Church as well as in the pulpit, since men and women need each other. Christ has set us free. "If the Son therefore shall make you free, ye shall be free indeed" (John 8:36), free to work as a team ministry. Men and women complement each other in a team. This does not always have to be a husband-wife team. The team ministry plan for husband and wife and family would differ according to individual callings and gifts of grace.

In Genesis 3:15, we note that the curse put upon the serpent included a spirit of enmity between the woman and the serpent. This has been experienced down through the ages in the old controversy between men and women. Many inferiority complexes are a result of this spirit affecting both men and women. We can claim our deliverance from this enmity. Christ has paid the price for us all. There is no need for man or woman to undermine the opposite sex in the spiritual or the natural.

Man must have his expression as a man for the Lord and be free to express it in Christ to His glory. Woman must have her expression as a woman for the Lord and be

The Promise of Ministry to Women

free to express herself in Christ to His glory. "Stand fast therefore in the liberty wherewith Christ hath made us free, and be not entangled again with the yoke of bondage" (Gal. 5:1).

2
The Many-Faceted Ministry of Women

Like a beautiful diamond, the ministry of women has many facets. Let us look briefly at a few notes on many women mentioned in the Bible to help us see the variety of their ministrations. The Lord has a many-membered ministry for women as well as for men, because people are different and because the Lord loves variety, as we have seen. What a beautiful thing it is to see the touch of the Master's hand in His Body of believers. We all need one another. We all make up for one another's lack.

Women-to-Women Ministries (Exod. 15:20-21)
Many women's ministries are mentioned in both the Old and New Testaments, but often today we fail to recognize them because they are spoken of in the Bible in the terminology of the day. Some women are referred to as ministers, but many others, who are in fact ministers, are spoken of under some other name. Or perhaps no particular name is given to their gift.

WOMEN IN MINISTRY TODAY

Strictly speaking, of course, all believers are priests to God and hence "ministers" in one sense of the word. Some carry out ministry gifts of a special kind; others use more general gifts and talents. But all are ministers really. The United Church of North Australia has recently recognized this. It calls all believers who are serving the Lord "ministers." Those whose particular ministry is preaching or teaching are called "ministers of the Word," but there are many other kinds of ministers. Those who are full time and receive a salary are called "stipendiary ministers," but they are not held to be any higher than those who support their ministries with ordinary jobs.

We recognize many kinds of women ministers in the Bible by the fruits of their gifts. We will look at some of these references, using our Bible dictionaries, our commentaries, and our concordances. As mentioned elsewhere, I make it a rule always to check the Greek and Hebrew word meanings with those who have earned the right to comment on these words. Thank God, I have close friends who are fully qualified to give assistance in all these matters.

Let us take a brief look at three examples in the Bible and see the different expressions used today to describe the ministries involved.

Different Types of Gifts

So far as we can judge, the New Testament teaches that there are a variety of gifts, and that these are of different types. Different Greek words are used to describe them. In some cases they fit in with natural talents, but this is

The Many-Faceted Ministry of Women

not always the case.

We learn in 1 Corinthians 12 that every believer has some gift, some manifestation of the Spirit. These are really spiritual operations that God works through us, and they are mainly intended not for our benefit (not like a Christmas or birthday present!) but for the edification of the congregation. Some people may manifest different spiritual operations at different times, as the need arises. For the most part, these gifts (see Romans 12) are used within the local church.

But in Ephesians 4:10-12, we read of somewhat different gifts, designated by another Greek word. We can call these the ministry gifts, given by the ascended Christ to His Church. These are specially anointed ministries, tailor-made to fit the recipient's personality and life. They are usually exercised among a wider segment of the Body of Christ than the local congregation affords.

These ministry gifts are in fact people; those gifted men and women are themselves Christ's gifts to His Church. We cannot really separate them from their ministry. Such people usually minister in depth and breadth, giving much of their time, or full time, to this work. They are not better or more worthy than Christians with a spiritual gift operating in his or her life, for all gifts are given us by God's unmerited favor. They are just exercising different kinds of gifts, though the dividing line is not always clear, nor need it be.

Apostles and prophets head the list of ministry gifts in Ephesians 4. The ministries of apostles and prophets are much misunderstood today and when they occur, they usually carry a different name. But they can be recognized by their fruits.

Evangelists, pastors, and teachers are ministry gifts which we understand better. People can exercise ministries in each of these areas, either as full ministry gifts, or as spiritual gifts or ministries. The same is true of the prophet, though the ministry of an apostle seems to be confined to a ministry gift.

For example, we have two kinds of pastoral gift—the local pastor or elder with a gift for pastoral care, and the ministry-gift pastor, who ministers with a shepherd's concern to the wider Body, and who often becomes a pastor of pastors.

In the same way, there are local evangelists who operate mainly within the outreach sphere of the local church, using their gift as called upon, and there are specially anointed, ministry-gift evangelists, who preach the gospel over a much wider area. Billy Graham is a good example of a ministry-gift evangelist.

Again, we have the local teacher whose gift in teaching God's Word brings regular blessing and edification to the local church and sometimes beyond it. We also have the ministry-gift teacher, whose special anointing puts him in demand all over an area, a nation, or even around the world as a teacher, and as a teacher of teachers.

Women Are Included!

Notice that nowhere are we told that some gifts or some ministry gifts are for men only. There is no suggestion in the New Testament that women receive a different

The Many-Faceted Ministry of Women

set of gifts from men. We are told that all believers have some ministry and that God has set special ministry gifts within the Church, as well. All are supposed to develop the gifts they have, stir them up and use them under the properly constituted authority of those God has told to lead the various parts of His Body. They do not minister in their own authority but in God's authority and under the control of the visible Church. All the gifts are open to women and to men.

But there are some who are reluctant to admit this. They fear the old myth that if women are allowed to do anything, they will become "aggressive" or "take over." Because of this they fail to allow women their fair share of ministry opportunities, and a sad loss to the whole Body is the result. Women themselves often hold back from discovering and using their gifts in the false fear that this would be unladylike. Many women sell themselves and their sisters short, and suffer from inferiority complexes and timidity. They fail to take the place God wants to give to all His people in ministry. Of course, women have sometimes made mistakes in ministry, but so have men!

Perhaps we are more prepared today than in the past in charismatic circles to admit that women can be prophetesses; we tend to think of this as just meaning the exercise of a spoken gift in a service. We have not realized that when a woman has the ministry gift of a prophetess, this means that, like a prophet, she often carries anointed governmental responsibility and authority under God.

A complete study of the book of Acts and other parts of

WOMEN IN MINISTRY TODAY

the New Testament will reveal the wide scope of women's ministries in the Body. Notice that Paul referred to the woman Priscilla and her husband, Aquila, as "my helpers in Christ Jesus" (Rom. 16:3; see also Acts 18:2, 18, 26). The word means "fellow workers"—they are both recognized as ministers together, without distinction in rank. It is interesting that Priscilla is mentioned first. Usually the husband would be named first; this indicates how well-known Priscilla was as a minister of Christ. Indeed, her name has been found carved in the catacombs of Rome, where they came to call her a saint for her blessed ministry.

Many commentaries suggest that the "elect lady" referred to in 2 John was in fact a pastor who had a church meeting in her home. Most of the early congregations met in homes. The Greek words applied to her mean "chosen, excellent, preeminent" and "lady" (the feminine form of *kurios*, "lord"). John is referring to an honorable woman who appears to have been more than simply a godly mother.

Apostles are still in our midst today, too, though they are not usually called by that title. Some believe that all apostles ceased in New Testament times, but there is nothing in the Bible to show that this ministry gift ceased. Certainly the original twelve apostles were unique, but there were many other apostles in the early Church, including Paul, so that care had to be taken to distinguish between true and false apostles. (This would hardly have been a problem if the only apostles were the twelve!) Paul sends his greetings to one, Junia, who is "of note among the apostles" (Rom. 16:7). As Junia is a feminine name, this could very well mean that she was an apostle, though some commentators have resisted that possibility by saying that Junia was a male apostle with a woman's name!

The basic meaning of the word apostle is "sent one," someone sent out by God and the Church to proclaim the good news. The Latin equivalent to this Greek word is "missionary," which means the same thing. Not all who go out today as missionaries have the ministry gift of an apostle, but we may be sure that some of them do. Apostles may work on the home front or overseas. The apostolic gift breaks open new places, breaks up new ground for the gospel and establishes God's work, much as Paul did. Often the power of God accompanies this ministry in signs and miracles and with anointed teaching.

We recognize the various gifts by their fruits, even if they are given modern labels. Apostles may be called missionaries or church planters. Prophets may be called evangelists or teachers, revelation preachers, ministers, or pastors.

The prophet, as we have seen, has a variety of aspects to his or her calling. Prophets bring fresh vision or warning to the Church, in revealing the mind and will of God to the people. Prophets often have an anointed teaching ministry as well, and they bring to the people with authority and love the revelation of God's word and of what we are in Christ. Prophets usually manifest discernment and other gifts of the Spirit as a part of their ministry.

There are many beautiful ministries that women can exercise within the rich and varied framework of God's

WOMEN IN MINISTRY TODAY

Word. They can be involved in meeting all the needs of God's children. No gift is denied them.

Let us summarize, with the help of some Bible aids, some of the ministries available to God's daughters.

3
Women in the Bible and Today

Summary of Some Women's Ministries

1. In the Gospels we read of several women messengers who proclaimed the good news (Matt. 28:1-10; Luke 24:9-11; John 4:28-30; 20:16-18). Some of these were evangelists.

2. In Acts 2:14-21 and Joel 2:28-31, God predicted He would pour out His Spirit upon women and they would prophesy. "To prophesy" means "to speak to men to edify, exhort, and comfort" (1 Cor. 14:3). "He that prophesieth, edifieth the church" (1 Cor. 14:4). Prophesying is for the church and general public (1 Cor. 12:1-31; 14:1-6, 12, 24-26, 29-33). So women can be prophetesses.

3. In Acts 21:8-9 it is clear that Philip's four daughters were prophetesses and ministers with anointed revelation, having teaching and preaching abilities in God's Word.

4. In Romans 16 we have record of a number of

women servants of the Lord in various churches: Phebe (verses 1-2), Priscilla (verses 3-5), Mary, Tryphena, Tryphosa, Persis, and Junia (verse 6-15) are mentioned as laborers in the Lord. These women were using various gifts.

5. In Philippians 4:2, Euodias and Syntyche are mentioned as being leaders of the church at Philippi.

6. Corinthian women prophesied and prayed in church (1 Cor. 11:4-5), so the Scriptures in 1 Corinthians 14:34-35 that are used to condemn women preachers cannot refer to preaching. It refers to disturbances in church services, such as chattering and women calling out questions to their husbands. In 1 Corinthians 14:35 and 1 Timothy 2:11-15, Paul is not condemning women preachers. Rather he condemns (men or) women preachers who are carnal (sense-ruled) and who take authority over their husbands (by an argumentative, overbearing spirit) and go against the laws and customs of their nation. Both men and women at Corinth were permitted to pray and prophesy, but were regulated by the laws of wisdom and *agape* love in doing so (1 Cor. 14:24-32).

7. In 1 Corinthians 12 Paul compares the Church to a human body and mentions nine gifts of the Spirit, including the gift of prophecy, for all the members of the Body of Christ, men and women. Other gifts are mentioned elsewhere in Scripture.

8. Women were used of God in the Old Testament days as prophetesses (Exod. 15:20; Judg. 4:4; 2 Kings 22:14; 2 Chron. 34:22; Neh. 6:14; Isa. 8:3). The law

Women in the Bible and Today

had made provision for women to make sacrifices, attend feasts, and make vows (Deut. 12:11-19; Lev. 27).

It is wonderful to see the touch of the Master's hand as He fashions and artistically creates a great variety of characters to exercise ministries in the Body of Christ.

Ministry and Character

Following on pages 34 and 35 is a selection from God's Word of various women's ministries and a summary of the character traits that accompany those ministries. We cannot separate a person's individuality from her ministry, for they are all one.

Some Qualities of the Ideal Woman

"The Ideal Woman" ("Who can find her?")
  Proverbs 31:10-31
  The ideal wife
    to her husband.
  The ideal woman
    in character.
  The ideal mother
    to her children.
  The ideal woman minister
    to the Body of Christ
    and to the unsaved.

We cannot expect to attain to the qualities of the ideal woman by ourselves, of course; only the power of Christ

Ministries	Character Type	Bible verse
Hospitality	A warm, open-hearted, considerate woman.	2 Kings 4:10
Kindness to the poor	Loving and considerate, respecting God and the poor.	Proverbs 31:20
Ministry unto the Lord	A very devoted, affectionate, loyal woman.	Luke 7:38
Deaconess of the church	A radiant, honest, faithful-in-all things, blameless woman.	Romans 16:1
Woman elder, pastor	A most excellent and honorable, temperate, capable, blameless, compassionate woman.	2 John 1:1-6
Apostolic ministry	An energetic, capable, patient, sound-minded, faith-motivated woman.	Romans 16:3, 7
Prophetess and national leader (Deborah)	An aggressive, busy, enthusiastic, inspirational, courageous, faithful, mother in Israel, gifted with a prophetic command, compassionate woman.	Judges 4:14
Prophetess (Miriam)	A dramatic, imaginative, poetic, inspirational, out-going, thoughtful, joyful woman.	Exodus 15:20
Prophetess (Anna)	A gracious, dedicated, appreciative, inspirational, revelational, gifted woman.	Luke 2:36
Prophetesses (Phillip's four daughters)	They were supernaturally illuminated expounders and preachers with inspirational qualities and intuitive abilities. Sensitive, passionate, active, self-expressive, compassionate, friendly, bright, gifted women. The above qualities would be divided among the personalities of the four daughters.	Acts 21:8-9
Evangelist	A generous, affectionate, emotional, friendly, out-going woman.	John 4:28-29
A ministry of love	A warm, gentle, beautiful, considerate, protective, vivacious woman. Loyal friend.	Genesis 35:8

Ministries	Character Type	Bible Verse
Dressmaker	A woman of kindness, love and devotion with practical deeds of love.	Acts 9:36-41
Businesswoman	An active, enterprising, efficient, dependable, hospitable woman.	Acts 9:36-41
Homemaker	A careful, conscientious, idealistic, thorough woman.	Luke 10:40
Woman chosen of God	A notable, gentle, devoted, pure, holy woman of faith.	Luke 1:30-38
A capable woman	A trustworthy, proficient, thrifty, versatile, watchful woman.	Proverbs 31:16
Ideal mother	Dependable, understanding, wise, joyful, kind, merciful, prudent, considerate.	Proverbs 31:15, 27—29
Ambitious woman	An enthusiastic, restless attitude, with a strong drive; a courageous, admirable, fair-minded adventurous type.	Numbers 12:1-2; Judges 4:4-24
Woman-to-woman ministry	A joyful, exuberant, friendly, out-going attitude; an inspirational, edifying, faith-flowing ministration.	Exodus 15:20-21
Church workers	Devoted, faithful, blameless, compassionate, temperate, capable, honorable.	Romans 16:1-2; Acts 18:26; Philippians 4:3
Praise, worship, songs in the Spirit	Women of all character types.	Ephesians 5:18-19
Woman of wisdom	Open-minded, positive, cautious, generous, witty.	1 Kings 10:1-13
Woman of faith	A positive, very determined woman, but may be shy nevertheless.	Matthew 9:20-22
A good mother	Sincere, truthful, concerned; has protective qualities, strong morals, and endurance, active faith and love; responsible, unselfish, considerate, warm-hearted.	2 Timothy 1:5

WOMEN IN MINISTRY TODAY

in us can develop such qualities in our lives. However, it is profitable to meditate on the qualities in Proverbs 31, so we can seek Christ to develop them in our lives. Some qualities to meditate upon:
1. morally clean (verse 10)
2. invaluable (verse 10)
3. trustworthy (verse 11)
4. inherently good and true (verse 12)
5. ingenious and proficient (verse 13)
6. thrifty and industrious (verse 14)
7. dutiful and considerate (verse 15)
8. versatile, judicious, aggressive in a good sense (verse 16)
9. tireless, healthy, and courageous (verse 17)
10. joyful, efficient (verse 18)
11. watchful, cautious, a woman minister (verse 18)
12. thrifty and skillful (verse 19)
13. charitable, benevolent, adventurous (verse 20)
14. generous, merciful, a woman evangelist (verse 20)
15. fearless, provident (verse 21)
16. clever at decorating and furnishing; a homemaker (verse 22)
17. refined in taste, inspirational (verse 22)
18. respected, popular (verse 23)
19. industrious, a prosperous businesswoman (verse 24)
20. dependable, honest (verse 25)
21. confident, hopeful (verse 25)
22. wise, discreet, expounding God's Word (verse 26)
23. kind, understanding, inspirational preacher (verse 26)
24. prudent, practical (verse 27)

Women in the Bible and Today

25. energetic, active, enthusiastic (verse 27)
26. ideal wife and mother (verse 28)
27. honored by her family and the church (verses 27—28)
28. excels in virtue (verses 28-29)
29. God-fearing, humble (verse 30)
30. deserving, successful (verse 31)
31. honored by the public (verse 31)

Many of these qualities mentioned in Proverbs 31 are also important qualities involved in the exercise of the ministry gifts. We see here some of the qualities needed by an apostle, a deaconess, a teacher, a woman pastor, a prophetess, an elder, or an evangelist. Christian women can be any of these, and the same qualities they require for a fulfilling ministry in the home are needed in ministry in the body of Christ also. But don't be discouraged if you cannot be all these things! Seek out and develop those good qualities and gifts God has given you, and expect Christ to live His life in and through you.

Some Special Distinctions Accorded to Women in the Bible
Women were:
  Last at the cross (Mark 15:47)
  First at the tomb (John 20:1)
  First to proclaim the resurrection (Matt. 28:8)
  First preacher to the Jews (Luke 2:37-38)
  Attended the first prayer meeting (Acts 1:14)
  First to greet Christian missionaries (Acts 16:13)
  First European convert (Acts 16:14)

WOMEN IN MINISTRY TODAY

Women in Our Day

Here are just a few names to encourage and inspire you:

Dr. Henrietta Mears was one of the greatest Bible teachers of our times. Her work among youth at the First Presbyterian Church in Hollywood, California, was of lasting significance. She was an excellent Bible teacher and founded Gospel Light Publications, one of the foremost evangelical publishing houses in the United States.

Adelaide Locher had a beautiful ministry. God sent her forth to bring light in the midst of great suffering.

Mary Slessor was known as the White Queen of Calabar in Africa. She was a missionary who worked amid great hardships. Her ministry affected many lives for Christ.

Kathryn Kuhlman, who died not so long ago, was a woman with a wonderful ministry of faith and power. Her big meetings in Pittsburgh and in Los Angeles and her TV appearances brought blessing, healing, and salvation to multiplied thousands. Her books blessed many more, and the Kathryn Kuhlman Foundation supplied money to assist many worthwhile Christian projects—Christian colleges, care of needy children, and so forth.

Rev. Jean Darnall had a remarkable and valued ministry for many years in Angelus Temple, Los Angeles. She ministers in Foursquare and other Full Gospel work in many parts of the world.

Corrie ten Boom, a Dutch woman with tremendous

faith and authority in Christ, has blessed the lives of thousands through her speaking, writing, and personal ministry. This brave woman survived internment in a Nazi concentration camp during the war, where many terrible things were done to the prisoners. She saw her own sister die in this situation, neglected in her need by a callous nurse. Corrie ten Boom later met this nurse again, was enabled to love her through God's great love in her life, and led this poor woman to Christ. She has written of the remarkable miracles of God's care and provision during those dark days. If you haven't read her books, such as *The Hiding Place, Amazing Love,* and *A Prisoner and Yet,* you should certainly do so. They will be an inspiration to you. In her later years, Miss ten Boom has been used of God in a ministry to Christians in Eastern Europe. She is a Spirit-filled believer.

Mother Teresa is a famous Catholic nun who, with other sisters, devotes her life to the poorest of the poor in the terrible slums of Calcutta, India. She spends much time with those who are dying of starvation or disease and who have lost all hope in this life, caring for and comforting them and pointing them to Jesus.

Time would fail us to tell of the many women God has wonderfully used, some in quiet ways, others in very public positions, some working in teams with their husbands, others renouncing the joys of a home and family to serve God more completely. *Miss Eugenia Price* is a well-known Christian writer and speaker to women. In Austrialia, there are many fine Christian women working as speakers in the Christian Women's Conventions, sometimes traveling to remote areas in order to reach women who usually have little fellowship. *Miss Jean Raddon* is just one of these. She was a missionary in Nepal and now works full time with the conventions. Women have founded missionary societies, as did for example *Mrs. L.W. Long,* who commenced the Aborigines Inland Mission of Australia in 1905, and *Miss Young,* who started the work of the South Sea Evangelical Mission.

Did you know that far more women have served on the mission fields of the world over the years than have men? Many go with their husbands to foreign lands and labor lovingly for the Lord, but many more go as single workers, knowing that in doing this, they are probably denying themselves the opportunity to meet eligible young men and settle down to a normal marriage and home life. There are few single men willing to make this sacrifice, though some do. Far more single women have gone out, often to dangerous and difficult places, to serve the Lord.

In the churches here at home, too, it is very often the womenfolk who carry the weight of the work and raise or contribute much of the money needed. Far more women than men attend church regularly overall, though unfortunately, as yet, they often have too little say in church affairs and in decision making. This is gradually changing, as more and more churches are ordaining women pastors, elders, evangelists, and other workers. God is blessing the efforts of these women.

PART TWO

The Governing Principle of All Ministries

We must remind ourselves of 1 Corinthians 13, "Though I speak with the tongues of men and of angels and have not charity *[love]*, . . . I am nothing." Whatever gifts we may have, if love is not there, they are of no more value than a hollow gong or a clanging cymbal. Without love, all is empty and worthless. *Agape* love is the greatest thing in the world, the most balancing factor. Nothing compares with it. Paul tells us to follow this principle. It will produce a symphony of God's divine love, and in the life of a woman it will produce a beautiful melody, a harmony of grace through our Lord.

In the chapter referred to, we can see Paul's description of the ingredients of *agape* love. It endures long and is patient and kind. It never boils over with jealousy or envy. It is not boastful and doesn't display itself in a haughty manner. It is never conceited, arrogant, or inflated with pride, nor does it have bad manners. It does not insist on its own way—not even on its rights. *Agape* love is not self-seeking, touchy, fretful, or resentful. It takes no account of evil done to it and pays no attention to a suffered wrong. It does not rejoice in injustice and unrighteousness when these befall someone else, but is glad when right and truth prevail.

We can contrast these qualities of *agape* love with natural, human love (called *phileo* in Greek).* *Phileo* lacks these enduring qualities. We have all seen how often and how easily mere human love breaks down. The divorce rate is one in four in many places and in some areas even one in two. And there are many unhappy marriages where no divorce is sought, as well! What a difference we see in the home founded on God's love! *Agape* is able to bear up under anything that comes, but *phileo* easily breaks down. *Agape*'s hopes never fade under any circumstances; this is a God-given, not a natural, quality. *Phileo* cannot endure many troubles without weakening in its hope. *Agape,* in fact, never fails. *Phileo* easily fails. *Agape* is unselfish; its principle is to give and to keep on giving. *Phileo* is based on getting. God's love in us can transform life, home and family relationships. This is one of the greatest open secrets of all time!

The wonderful truth is that when we are born again, we are born of *agape* love. It comes to dwell in our hearts. But we need to understand this, and to *believe* that God is working His love in us. Faith activates it. We need to realize that we cannot depend on natural human love. We

---

*Agape is pronounced a-gah′-pay. *Phileo* is pronounced feel-eh′-oh.

The Governing Principle of All Ministries

can only live by God's love as we receive its truth. I found this revelation of divine love to be the greatest adventure of my life, the most powerful governing principle of my ministry. Let this love be your aim—in your family life, in your other ministries, and in all of life.

1
The Way of the Cross

I have sought to approach this subject of the Spirit-filled woman in ministry with unbiased attitudes, allowing Scripture to speak to us. I have sought the wisdom and viewpoints of scholars and famous Bible teachers, and have conferred with ministers around the world. The centrality of love has been stressed.

Now I would like to share some of my personal experiences. This principle, that God deals with us by the way of the Cross, is very important. We must pause here to look at it. *All* those with ministry gifts, men and women, will find God deals with them by way of the Cross. Our concern at present, however, is with women.

Let us each ask ourselves, "Do I believe that I am called and chosen of God to exercise a particular ministry gift?" If so, we must then ask another question: "Am I prepared to bear the Cross through the dealings of God in my life?"

It is true, as we have said, that our ministries as women can be very beautiful. But we must not look at them through rose-colored glasses. Our ministries are not fragile, delicate things which cannot stand up to real-life situations. They must be strong. After all, we are in a great battle between good and evil, and a war is no place for fragile people without strength. God has to prepare us for the battle. Our ministries must be tried and true. If we cannot face this fact, we should forget ministry.

Let me share my little story with you. It is the story of all women ministers who are truly called. Circumstances may differ, though the principles will remain constant. To tell you my whole life story would fill several books. God has dealt wonderfully with me. Rather, I will try to draw out the golden thread which is our concern at present.

My husband and I are both Australians. My church background was Baptist and my husband's background was Christian Brethren. We ministered throughout Australia and New Zealand for eight years, then attended Crusade Bible College in Adelaide, South Australia, for further training in ministry. After graduation, we continued to minister and founded several new churches and convention centers as God brought people into His salvation and blessing. We pastored in several centers and also conducted a school of evangelism. Then we left Australia for a time and ministered in other lands, particularly in the United States and Canada, but also in India, Japan, Hong Kong, Haiti, and a number of other nations.

Believe it or not, I had been given up by medical specialists in my late teens. I suffered from so many complaints that they believed I could not live. I had chronic

The Way of the Cross

asthma, and I had suffered from pleurisy and pneumonia, bleeding lungs, and kidney troubles. Furthermore, I was mentally tormented day and night with fear of rejection and great insecurity. I felt I was cut off from God as I gasped for air. It seemed I was allergic to most of the drugs the doctors administered to relieve my asthma; these only increased my suffering. For years I suffered physical torture and mental agony.

I had cried to God for help and searched the Bible for His promises. I began to see these were real, and I would take hold of the promises of healing as best I could. Then a measure of relief would come—it was a little like heaven. But it usually did not last. I would again be plunged into the fires of suffering. This happened over and over again for several years. I was tempted to denounce God's promises, but His great grace always reached down and prevented this. Often God called me to minister, but I refused to listen. I believed the Bible did not permit women to exercise ministries and, anyway, I was too ill and had too great a fear of rejection.

Nevertheless, the Word of God kept me alive, quite literally. And after a time, that Word began to break down the power of fear and sickness. Once I had a vision of Christ. I shall never forget the love in His face. He showed me that God was dealing with my life by the way of the Cross, and that there would also be an experience of "resurrection life" for me. He showed me this through revelation truths in His Word.

Little by little, slowly but surely, these truths began to bring deliverance. I realized that the truth which delivered me would through my ministry bring deliverance and enlightenment to others in the Body of Christ.

My husband meantime had accepted his call from God to minister, with much less struggle than I had had. God was using him. Before long God's Word was revealed to both of us in a new way. My healing began and I knew God was moving. He was dealing with me by way of the Cross, because He always deals in this way with those He chooses to minister. The Cross takes many forms, but it is always there. My husband and I began to understand this. He had had his crosses, too.

In previous years, we had been deeply in bondage to a very legalistic assembly. Satan loves to put God's people in chains! We had followed the letter rather than the spirit of the law, and had sat under a ministry of condemnation for a long time. This had been hindering my release from suffering. It was about this time, just as my healing was beginning, that God reached out His mighty hand to deliver us from this legalism. He helped us recognize the bondage we were in, and that God's children do not need to live that way. He led us out into liberty and into a ministry which majored on righteousness rather than condemnation. He showed us the wonderful revelation of who we are—not in ourselves, as sinners, but in Christ, as His redeemed sons and daughters.

With our joyous, new-found liberty came a fresh challenge. God wanted Cliff and me to move out more for Him. I was being healed. That meant I would be able to share in ministry with my husband. But God challenged me again with the way of the Cross. Was I willing to for-

The Way of the Cross

sake the normal benefits enjoyed by most women—a home of our own, the security of a regular income, material possessions, popularity, nearness to loved ones?

I had to count the cost of moving into evangelistic ministry. People think you are very odd if you sell your home and means of livelihood and move out by faith in ministry. I would be rejected as Christ was rejected. It was the religious people who crucified Christ, and it is often religious people who persecute some of Christ's servants still. But God's servants must be prepared to forsake all if He so calls and to put aside concerns for worldly pleasures, gains, and reputation. This does not mean He wants us to be irresponsible, as some have been. It does mean that He expects us to listen carefully to His voice and to obey Him, whatever the cost.

When I had settled these things in my heart, there came still other testings. God purges our ministry of anything false. At one time my dear husband became hard in his heart towards me—something rare for him. You can imagine how this hurt me. But God used this to forge a forgiving heart in me and to teach me humility. I learned that we cannot depend on any person, not even on our spouse, but on God alone. People, even the dearest, can fail us. Or they may be taken from us. Our expectation is from Him—the Lord. Do you see how God teaches us, not simply by imparting academic knowledge to us, but also by working His graces in us through the circumstances and hindrances of life?

I felt God had called me to minister, but still the way to preaching was not made open. I constantly met men who

WOMEN IN MINISTRY TODAY

were rigidly against women preachers. God showed me that this would work grace in me. I would have to wait on His timing for my ministry to come forth. Often it seemed as if some men would deliberately undermine my confidence. They would ignore me, or trivialize me, recognizing only my husband. I was just part of the furniture! Have you ever felt this way? Of course it is not God's will for men to treat women in this way. But God allowed it to happen, to develop *agape* love in me. My ministry would be worthless without that love!

In those days, when every door was closed to me simply because I was a woman, faith was born in my heart. It was born by way of *closed doors!* When we see the doors open, we do not need to exercise faith. God wanted me to trust Him to develop in me not only the calling He had given but the *means for carrying it out*. To receive no recognition of my ministry was a wonderful way of dealing with my pride and developing grace and love in me. All this was God's preparation for what was to come.

For a number of years, I waited quietly for God to open His doors. During that time, my first concern had to be for my five children. This was an important ministry in itself. My husband and family became the first fruits of my ministry. That will be the case for many women. We were often on the move, and it is not easy to care for young children under those circumstances. We had little, but God always sufficiently provided. We learned many lessons of dependence on God. I was able to share in my husband's ministry in many ways, but I knew there was more to come.

God quickened to me a special thought: *The gift will*

The Way of the Cross

make a way for itself under God's providential hand. I rested in this assurance, and allowed the Lord to use all circumstances to His glory.

Eventually the time came when we were led to a fellowship of ministers who gladly received us. They too had come to see the difference between legalism and grace. We fitted in beautifully with this fellowship. They were not completely open to women ministers, though they were much more open than most in recognizing God's gifts to women as well as to men. They had never accepted and ordained a woman pastor, but they had welcomed a fine woman preacher and allowed her to minister several times in their midst. These folks believed that a ministry is known by its fruits.

I realized God was leading me, but it was necessary for me to walk in humility and in love to hear His voice. I saw that He wants to develop these qualities in His ministers. Soon afterwards, I began to realize that it is not recognition from people that should be my main concern. I had to be thinking more about how to please God and help others. When I got more involved in serving others, things began to happen. God showed me that I should simply begin serving Him in every way which *was* open to me, however simple and humble, and to forget about recognition. He began to bless *when I forgot about myself and my recognition.* Have you ever noticed that interesting little verse at the end of the book of Job—chapter 42, verse 10—"And the Lord turned the captivity of Job, when he prayed for his friends: also the Lord gave Job twice as much as he had before"? Job had to get his eyes off himself and think of others too, before blessing and deliverance came!

When I was least thinking about it, God began to open doors for me to preach. Gradually, recognition did come to me. But God had to put me in the right frame of mind first!

I wonder if one of my sisters, reading this, is in a similar position? You feel God has called you and given you a gift, but the doors all seem closed. Forget about your own recognition and think of others. *Start where you are.* Enter the doors which are open, however small. Take the chance to go and pray with a lonely shut-in, to visit an elderly person or someone who is ill, to teach Sunday school, or whatever God shows you. If you can write or draw, begin using those talents quietly for the Lord. Give yourself to the important ministry in the home. Become an intercessor. Give to God's work. Offer hospitality to visiting believers and ministers. These are real ministries in themselves. If God has more for you, *the gift will make way for itself,* in God's good time. Be patient and attentive to the work God is trying to do *in you.* Even if all doors seem closed and everyone around you is opposed to women's ministries, look to God in faith, and see what happens! There may be times when a holy boldness is required, but God will show you when. Wait on Him.

But to continue with my story. The fellowship of ministers with whom we were meeting included some renowned teachers of the Word. They formed a rather large charismatic fellowship. We were glad to be identified with them. One day they approached me to ask if I would

The Way of the Cross

like to be ordained—their first woman minister! Imagine my joy! I accepted this as an honor and responsibility from the Lord. My husband was also very happy for me to accept this. Cliff is the kind of man who is secure enough in his own manhood and ministry not to be jealous or fearful of his wife's ministry. Rather, he was glad that my gifts were recognized and that our opportunities to minister together as a team would be enhanced and increased. This is how a good Christian husband should be—happy for his wife to move ahead, eager to encourage her, generous enough in nature to accept his wife's ministry and rejoice in her opportunities. Certainly such an attitude is included in the command that husbands love their wives as Christ loved the Church, for Christ is always eager that His people develop their personalities and ministries as far as possible. He loves to see this. Some husbands, unfortunately, have allowed a false pride to make them jealous of any achievements their wives may enjoy. But God is able to break down this too.

The Value of God's Dealings

I think you can see in my experiences the importance of submitting to God's dealings in our lives. Because God will cause the gift to make a way for itself, we need never strive or struggle to be recognized. We can allow God to use circumstances which appear to *hinder* our calling, so that they in fact help *develop* it. He wants His servants to learn grace, love, faith, humility, and a forgiving heart. Only then can these qualities flow out to bless others. Graciousness can flow from us, and love can throb in each word we minister. Tenderness and understanding will develop new richness and depth in our ministry. Through a submissive and kind heart, we can minister to others. How cold, hard, and dry is a ministry which lacks these qualities. God has to lead us by the way of the Cross!

It may be that fewer people today are opposed to women's ministries than was the case in my younger days. However, in some circles we see a return to legalism on this matter among charismatics and other evangelicals. Some seem to be just reacting to the extremes of some un-Christlike women, or to a generally more permissive society, which makes them fearful and leads them to draw back into hyperconservative shells instead of stepping out in bold faith. Whatever the reason, there are situations in which Christian women are being told their place is wholly in the home, and that if God ever gave them any ministry gifts at all, they are not meant to be used! (Did God make a mistake?) This is not at all like the busy woman in Proverbs 31. She was no shrinking violet. Rather, she was both a fine homemaker and a competent businesswoman, much involved in many things in the community and among the believers.

Some women are being put under terrible bondage again. They are told to put handkerchiefs on their heads when they pray, and never to participate in a church service at all. They are told to keep quiet all the time, and never to venture an opinion, follow an ambition, or be real people in their own right. How sad and how un-biblical! But here is an opportunity, sister, for faith! I know what you are going through, for I suffered it all, too.

But Jesus has a better plan for you. Listen to His voice, and let Him develop in you the attributes He wants. He will respond to your faith if you know the truth about women's ministries and trust in Him. He will not let you remain a "nothing" forever, but you must first renounce the concern about personal recognition from other people, as I had to do. God recognizes you as a valuable person in His sight, and that is enough to begin with.

Perhaps you move in circles where these problems do not exist. Many Christians today, fortunately, have more enlightened attitudes about women. Thank God, then, for the liberty you enjoy. But remember—God's principles for the development of His ministers remain the same. He still needs to take you the way of the Cross for you to be the kind of person He wants you to be. Some circumstances will block your way, and the Bible teaches you ought not to think this strange. Some people will stand against you, perhaps in your own family. But God uses these circumstances; it is important to understand this.

The Controversies Over the Charismatic Movement and Women Ministers

We all remember, if we have long been in the charismatic movement, the days when there was far greater controversy than now about the charismatic movement of the Spirit. Some of us came into the fullness of the Spirit amid great persecution—we lost friends and were considered followers of Satan by some! We were classed along with the cults, and "decent" Christians avoided us. People warned that we would end up on the spiritual scrapheap. Speaking in tongues was thought to be some kind of seance. Dark rumors were spread about pentecostals, who supposedly swore profusely in other tongues or who engaged in unspeakable immorality because of their dreadful teachings! It reminds us a bit of the early Christians, who were accused of being cannibals and atheists! Of course there were some of our number who merited some of the things which were said, but no more than did a number of noncharismatics.

We remember the old arguments against us: only very ignorant folk are pentecostals; those blessings were only for the apostolic age; charismatics are of the devil and immoral. The accusers were proven wrong. While some remain inalterably opposed, many who objected to us are now with us, and others have greatly tempered their opposition.

The controversy over women ministers has been similar. A few "proof texts" were taken out of context to bind up women so they could not exercise any significant ministry outside the home. The overall thrust of Scripture was forgotten. Attempts were made to show that because of Eve's deception all women forever afterwards are more easily deceived than all men. There was no room for redemption in these theories; women were to remain forever under the curse.

Those who have tried to reduce women to zombies in the Church have ignored God's choice of many women prophets, and of rulers like Deborah and teachers like Huldah. If these men were correct, we women would be better off living under the Old Testament Covenant, for

The Way of the Cross

God would have given us more opportunities for ministry then than He does now!

More subtly, those who try to bring us into bondage again cover their words with honey. Woman's totally subservient "role," they say, is really very beautiful, sweet, childlike, and godly. Many women believe it. But to rob a human being of dignity, personality, and the opportunity to exercise the free will God has given us can never be beautiful. To reduce a human being to almost a "thing," however nice we make that sound, is never God's will. To twist the Bible so that the priesthood of all believers means only the priesthood of men is terribly wrong and has done untold harm to the Church in the loss of many God-given ministries that could never be exercised. We do have cause for righteous indignation at some of these things. Yet we are not called to take revenge, but to wait on God and allow Him to show us the way out of bondage.

Large numbers of Christians now recognize that it is wrong to condemn women's ministries, just as large numbers now realize they were wrong to condemn the charismatic movement. Little by little, truth and fairness are winning out. God is having His way.

My husband and I have traveled to many lands on several continents in the past several years and have spoken to many ministers on this subject. We see wider acceptance of the charismatic movement than ever before, and we see many accepting the ministry of women also, despite the groups which remain opposed to it. Of course not all charismatics or all women ministers have acted in a Christlike fashion. Thus they have contributed to their own difficulties.

A True Story

We were told this story by a group of charismatic ministers in one of the nations we visited.

A fine Christian woman, whom we will call Anna May, is known for her beautiful, gracious spirit. She has an anointed ministry, and many are blessed as she preaches God's Word. She also has a ministry of teaching and a gift of healing, as well. She preaches and teaches with an authority not her own but God's (and conferred on her by the eldership of the church). Her presentation is seasoned with love and is full of life, and has produced fruit that remains. Any unbiased person would have to recognize that here is a God-given and God-blessed ministry. Anna May ministers at many crusades, conventions, luncheons, and the like. Her work is recognized and accepted by a large group of charismatic ministers, including many outstanding Bible teachers.

But predictably, there was a small group of male ministers who objected to Anna May's ministry. Their objections varied. Some said, "No woman speaker blesses me." Some declared it an insult to their manhood (how fragile their manhood must have been!). Others said they were embarrassed when a woman preached, and still others claimed it was "totally unscriptural."

Some, it seemed, felt it was their duty not only to reject what God was so obviously doing through Anna May but to "go and teach all nations" to reject women's ministries,

The Way of the Cross

as well. They tried to do so, but they met opposition from those who knew her ministry was of God. Those who were for Anna May showed the others that the Bible plainly demonstrated that women could minister.

Much discussion ensued, and the ministers who favored Anna May explained that the problem the other men had was in fact their problem, not Anna May's. They showed them that since the Bible was not against women ministering, their problem must be one of the following:

1. Misinterpretation of the Scriptures, which would make the Bible contradict itself, allowing women to minister yet forbidding it!
2. A problem in their own homes, so that they were unconsciously transferring their own problems with their wives or mothers to women in general.
3. A big male ego problem, which should have been nailed to the Cross.
4. A problem of general carnality, such as Paul mentioned in 1 Corinthians 3:1-6 (we suggest you pause and read these verses here). These verses speak for themselves.

This discussion produced some heart-searching! About half of the troubled ministers agreed that the problem was theirs. The others said that they didn't care if their attitudes were wrong. So far as they were concerned, women were only fit for home duties. A few were ready to admit that women could have ministries, but never ministry gifts. They could not prove this from the Word, however, which never suggests there is one group of gifts for men and another for women! They could hardly deny that the gift of prophetess was scriptural! Yet this gift carries with it a definite governmental authority, as does the gift of prophet—no distinction can be shown from the original languages. The gift also clearly carries with it preaching and public ministry. The negative group of ministers could only try to say lamely that such gifts were "not for today"—the very argument anticharismatics had so often used against them! They could give no reason for their claim. In the end, this negative group was just bypassed and disregarded. God continued to bless the ministry of Anna May.

We always encounter some opposition in doing God's work and should be prepared for this. When one person begins to speak doubts and disagreements, others soon follow. A little leaven leavens the whole lump. Yet often, no one has troubled to search out the matter thoroughly. They simply accept what others have told them. Numbers do not necessarily indicate truth, of course, and often large groups of very sincere people can be quite wrong. We must beware lest a few false brethren or legalists come into our group and persuade the whole church to believe a perverted gospel or a half lie (cf. Gal. 5:9).

2
Neither Male Nor Female in Christ Jesus (Galatians 3:28)

We have probably all wondered at some time about apparent contradiction in God's Word. We have appropriated certain Scriptures in our lives, while others seemed to say something else. For example, we see Scriptures which seem to subordinate women, and then we see a verse like Galatians 3:28, which tells us there is neither male nor female in Christ Jesus.

When we study "hermeneutics," the science and art of interpreting the Bible, we learn Scriptures approach things from different points of view, and that we must always read verses in their context. We know the Bible does not really contradict itself. It is important not to form doctrines just by grasping a few "proof texts" here and there, taken out of context. We need to look for the overall message of Scripture and for basic, underlying truths, which take precedence over incidental matters.

For example, the truth that we are justified by faith and not by works is a great underlying theme of the New

WOMEN IN MINISTRY TODAY

Testament. Therefore, when we read references to works in James, we do not take them out of context (e.g., James 2:24) and teach justification by works. A careful study of James will show us that James is insisting that true faith always results in good works, and that if a person's life shows only evil and no good works, we can rightly doubt that he has genuine faith or is truly saved. Likewise, there are many commands and examples in the Bible that we do not follow in detail, because we realize they were for a particular situation and were not meant for all time. There are other matters which show definite principles that are eternally valid, and we still hold to these.

A good method for studying the Bible is the one used in what is called biblical theology. When we approach the Bible this way, we let each Bible writer speak for himself, and then seek to put the whole together. We study, for example, the various writings of John all together, to see what they have to say on the matter at hand. Then we look at the two books by Luke, and then at Paul's writings. We seek to preserve the integrity and completeness of each author, rather than simply taking verses from many authors all over the Bible and throwing them together. We also look at the sayings of Christ as a whole.

Many Christians today believe that a statement such as "there is neither male nor female in Christ Jesus" is a statement of basic principle, more fundamental and enduring than some of the prohibitions put upon women in the particular circumstances of the Roman Empire. This is because the principle is in accord with so many of the great basic underlying teachings of Scripture. The

Neither Male Nor Female in Christ Jesus

Bible clearly teaches that man and woman are both made in the image of God. This gives them both true dignity, despite the Fall, and especially once Christ has redeemed them. The great themes of Creation, the Fall, and redemption support this claim. Nowhere in the basic gospel message is there any hint that woman is inferior or subordinate.

It is clear that woman was in no way subordinate to man at Creation; this came only as a result of the Fall. Redemption came to *deliver* us from the curse and from sin, not to press us down more than ever under its load, as some would do!

There is never a hint in any of Christ's words that woman is inferior or subordinate. Indeed, He spoke to women when other men would not. Jesus did not try to confine women to domestic duties only. In fact, when Martha was too preoccupied with housekeeping and entertaining Him, He rebuked her! He suggested that she emulate Mary, who gave first consideration to spiritual things. This is in accord with a basic and detailed passage which describes a worthy woman—the thirty-first chapter of Proverbs. Jesus must have known this passage. The ideal woman was *not* one who confined herself to domestic duties. She undertook these properly, but she had many other interests and occupations, as well, and certainly worked outside the home. (Working mothers take heart—the Bible does not condemn you for taking an outside job. But of course it indicates that you must, along with your husband, make certain your children are properly cared for at all times, and not left to their own devices while you are away.)

So the principle of Galatians 3:28 is fundamental to the New Testament. There is a basic equality in Christ between different races, between slaves and freemen (people of any status in life), and between the two sexes. This theme is so often stressed that we cannot doubt it. It took the Church some time to see the implications of this, and many still fail to see them. But the truth is there, just the same. Hallelujah!

The Context of Galatians

In accordance with good hermeneutics, let us study this passage in the wider context of Paul's message to the Galatian church. Something of his purpose in writing is seen in Galatians 1:6-7. Paul is concerned that the Galatians are too easily removed from grace to legalism, which is really "another gospel." God gave Paul a wonderful revelation of the difference between law and grace. Law held the central place in the Old Covenant, but it is grace which holds that place in the New Covenant.

The Law was like a teacher, used to bring us to Christ (Gal. 3:24). But in Christ, a new day had begun—the Day of Grace. The Law is now done away with (notice this concept in Galatians 4:30—"cast out"; in 2 Corinthians 3:7—"done away"; in Ephesians 2:15—"abolished"; in Hebrews 7:12—"changed"; in Hebrews 7:18—"disannulled"; and in Colossians 2:14—"blotted out").

Paul taught grace to the Galatians. He had preached justification by faith and they had accepted it. Now he declares that they had removed themselves from this firm position and followed after a false gospel. They still believed Christ died and rose again for their sins, but they now thought this only *partly* justified them. They still needed to do something else themselves.

Pause a moment and read in your Bible Galatians 2:4-5. False brethren had come in and brought them into bondage. These brethren were probably sincere, but they were wrong! The Galatian church was a non-Jewish church. As Gentiles, its members were not circumcised in Jewish fashion. Hence they were considered "people of the uncircumcision." In Jewish eyes, they were unclean, unsanctified, for Jews took great pride in this ceremony in their old religion. Such Jewish people came among the Galatians and persuaded the whole church to be circumcised in order to make their justification complete (verse 8). There was no problem when Jews who believed were circumcised according to the custom of all Jewish men of the time. The Lord allowed this, because it was not in itself a matter of great importance, and it would certainly make it much simpler for Jewish Christians to witness to other Jews. Why all the fuss, then, when the Galatians were circumcised?

Because they were Gentiles. This had not been their custom. They were doing this because someone had told them it was necessary for salvation. They were brought into bondage and the gospel was corrupted. Some today add to the gospel things which are in themselves good or neutral and try to make them necessary for salvation—baptism, the keeping of a particular day, the laying on of hands from a bishop, the Communion, or even speaking in tongues. But none of these things can be considered necessary for salvation, however desirable they may be. None can be legalistically forced on people as a part of their justification. That is why this circumcision error had become a dangerous heresy.

Man seems naturally prone to legalism. He is always wanting to make rules and to force people to carry out rituals and ceremonies. We see this in all pagan religions and in debased forms of Christianity as well. We must always guard against the wrong kind of legalism. (This is not to say that God has no standards for our conduct, though! Of course He does!)

In the remainder of his letter, Paul demonstrates the poor logic of the circumcision group. They must not frustrate God's grace by works of the Law, for that was to make Christ's work of no effect and to fall from grace (Gal. 5:4). Law and grace cannot mix. The Galatians might retain salvation, but their understanding would be darkened and they would lose their power to produce fruit. Chapter 4:21-31 answers these mixed teachings and is the climax of the book. You should pause and reread this passage here. It tells of the two covenants, one from Mt. Sinai, based on law, which leads to bondage, and one which is from Christ and is based on grace, which leads to liberty.

Hagar represented the covenant of the Law and the works of the flesh. Ishmael, her son, was not born miraculously, for Hagar was still quite young. But Sarah represents grace. She was very old when Isaac was born. Isaac was the miracle child, the child of promise. Ishmael was born of a mixture of faith and works (grace and law) in that Abraham was trying to fulfill God's promise himself, because he had come to doubt God. (He did this in a manner which was customary in those days, though it would be repugnant to us today.) In the same way, the Old Covenant was a mixture of faith and law. Notice that faith was present, even then, although people did not fully understand its significance. Abraham returned to real faith as he waited for God to give him the true child of promise. It was by his faith that he was justified, just as all God's people through the ages have been justified, but before the coming of Christ, people could not fully comprehend this. Thus the Law served as a schoolmaster, leading them to the eventual revelation of the Son of God.

Paul points out to the Galatians how they were in danger of reverting to the Old Covenant. Like Abraham they had to "cast out the bondwoman and her son." They needed to accept afresh the revelation of grace and liberty in Christ.

The Important Point

What does all this show us about the meaning of Galatians 3:28? The distinction between the circumcised and the uncircumcised was really *a distinction based on physical and social differences between people.* The Jews were one race of people and the Gentiles belonged to other races. The Jews looked down on the Gentiles traditionally. Circumcision reminded the Jews not only of their ancient covenant with God but also of their Jewish nationality, race, and culture.

WOMEN IN MINISTRY TODAY

The New Covenant, as can plainly be seen throughout the New Testament, makes no such distinctions. We are dealing here with a very basic theological principle. God is no respecter of persons. He chose the Jews not because they were better than other people or a larger nation (they were in fact a small nation, and often departed from God). He chose them, rather, simply as a vehicle for bringing His grace to *all* mankind. It was absolutely crucial to the New Covenant that people understand that the gospel is offered to all people without distinction. Racial barriers must fall down. Social and cultural barriers, even a barrier so great as that between slave and free citizen, must be broken down. And the many social distinctions between the sexes must also be broken down in Christ. Physical differences of race and of sex, Paul is saying, simply do not count anymore. Cultural differences and differences in social status do not count. Grace is offered to all! Peter's vision (see Acts 10) before he went to proclaim Christ to the Gentiles in the house of Cornelius was given to teach him the same lesson. He must not consider others unclean because they did not follow Jewish dietary laws and customs.

The social and legal status of slaves was as low as it could possibly be. The social and legal status of women was just about as low. The status of children also was very low. Only free men had any status in the Roman Empire, and then primarily those who were fortunate enough to hold Roman citizenship—the select few.

But the message of the gospel, we are clearly taught, takes no account of these things. The same offer of grace is to all. Jesus did not hesitate to speak to people of other races or to women or children. He elevated their status. He called children to himself and said, ". . . of such is the kingdom of heaven" (Matt. 19:14). We can understand that the social realities and injustices of the day were something the early Church had to live with, in practical everyday matters, and this comes out in the injunctions to minors, wives, and slaves. But the more enduring and more basic principle is the one we have seen Paul teach in Galatians: *There is no difference.* The full implications of that wonderful truth could not be worked out immediately in that society, but in time they have more and more come to the fore.

If there is no difference in the spiritual realm, there cannot ultimately be *any* difference between people in God's sight—in their value as persons, in the opportunities God wants them to have for ministry, or in any other way except the physical differences of race and sex. In this verse, God puts the differences between man and woman, so far as His gospel and His Church are concerned, *on the same level* as the differences between Jews and Gentiles, slaves and free men. In other words, they simply do not count. And in this is the charter of our freedom as women in Christ. Cultural differences and injustices will fall away as the gospel penetrates more of society and is better understood.

A Male Religion?

Notice here, too, that God himself is a Spirit. That means He is neither male nor female. We have to use human words to describe God, and the terms "Father" and "He" have been used. We have to call God either "he" or "she" in English, as these are the only two personal pronouns we have. We cannot call a person "it." In other languages the grammar is different. But it is important to understand that this is merely human language. We do not have higher language to describe God, though His Person really requires it. But it is quite wrong to believe that God is essentially a male! He is beyond our differences of sex, just as He is beyond our human differences of race. Christ came to earth as a man—He had to be either a man or a woman, and a man was the best choice in the culture of those times. But this still does not mean that God or the Trinity is *male!* A spirit is sexless.

There are some women today who do not wish to become Christians because they feel Christianity is really a religion mainly for men. God is male, Christ and the Holy Spirit are male, and men in the Church hold all the power while women have only low status. Unfortunately the Church often does look like that. But it is not meant to! Women are increasingly being given the place God intended. People are realizing that God is not a man any more than He is a woman—He is God! And there are attempts to change some of the Church language which is excessively masculine. These are good signs. Little by little, the truth of Galatians 3:28 is breaking through, and people are seeing the truth that sets them free in Christ. Let us obey Paul's injunction to "stand fast therefore in the liberty wherewith Christ has made us free, and be not entangled again with the yoke of bondage" (Gal. 5:1).

The "Yo-Yo" Problem

We often read Galatians 5:1 and sing the words. Do we understand what it means for us women? Very often, when Christian women begin to see this truth about themselves and their place in the Body of Christ, their hearts open up and they are thrilled. But the flesh naturally tends to fall back into bondage and legalism. Pretty soon, someone comes along and persuades them that the real teaching of the gospel for women is passivity, always taking the back seat, doing nothing outside the home, being just pretty dolls and foils to their husbands' egos and ministries. They quickly become entangled once again in bondage. And it may be harder than ever for them to break free the next time! They even believe that God has taught them to remain in bondage as a deep and wonderful lesson in humility, patience, self-effacement, or something of the kind. Christian women sometimes come in and out of bondage like a yo-yo, back and forth, unable to rest in their liberty in Christ.

Often women forget their liberty because some godly sister comes along, pats them on the shoulder and, with lots of kind, sincere, and apparently biblical language, woos them back into being nothings. Or they hear a thundering sermon from some well-known preacher, warning them that unless "God's order" is preserved in the home and the Church, the Church and the nation will crumble. This sounds fearful and convincing, and back into bondage falls our poor sister. Or perhaps she is having trouble in her home or some difficulties in her marriage . Almost invariably, the brother or sister who comes along to counsel her will suggest that perhaps she is not "submitting" to her husband (as if this were the source of all troubles) or that her husband is not "taking his place as head." Often, although they quote Scriptures, they mean something very different from what the Bible is saying. And the wife is soon reduced to tears, certain that any decision making, any assertion of her own personality, and any signs of being a real-life, full person must be wicked and the cause of all her problems.

If she has been exercising gifts, she may be told that she should stop, because when she ministers, she is "going against the Bible" and is detracting from her husband's (apparently fragile and selfish) manhood! His personality fulfillment and his full exercise of his ministry are rightly seen as important. But often the implication is that the fulfillment of her personality and ministry are not important—it does not matter what happens to her so long as her husband feels good and is successful in ministry. And many Christian women, being loving and gracious, really believe this.

The Wrong Answer: Masochism

It is of course true that we should "prefer one another in love" and be humble ourselves and submit one to another (which means, by the way, that husbands often are to submit to wives as well—all believers are to submit to one another, and no more is asked of the wife than is asked of all Christians to each other; see Ephesians 5:21).

Neither Male Nor Female in Christ Jesus

This is the point. Wives who are having difficulties at home rightly should look at themselves and be sure they are acting as love demands before they begin accusing their husbands. But there is often something in us women that is too ready to take the blame for everything, in what psychologists call a *masochistic* manner. There is a fine line between true, self-giving love based on a good, secure personality and a fearful masochism, which almost takes pleasure in being "walked upon" and badly treated, in always being the one to confess. Christian women are easily prone to masochism, which is unhealthy and based on an insecure personality. This is because they have so often been told that they are, in effect, inferior, unimportant, and supposed to hover like a ghost in the background, taking little initiative and living only in a vicarious manner through their husbands and children, instead of as full people in themselves, as God intended. It is also because they have so often been told they must be overly humble, and because they have too long sat under a ministry of guilt-producing condemnation.

Do you see our problem here? Men are less inclined to be subjected to this kind of trivialization and condemnation than women. If we become too masochistic, some men will take advantage of it. They will make little effort to confess their own faults, to show love, and to recognize male egotism. Masochism carried to an extreme can become a severe personality disorder in which one "likes" to be hurt, abused, and dominated by another person. The other person may sometimes develop correspondingly opposite behavior and delight in treating the other cruelly (this may be mental harm or physical harm). That is known as *sadism* and may occur in mild or severe forms. In its milder forms, a sadomasochistic relationship is quite common. It is usually unconscious, and the cruelty is generally mentally applied rather than showing itself in physical cruelty. Neither partner is likely to realize how dependent he or she is on the other. This can occur between any two people, but it frequently occurs in its milder forms between husbands and wives. It is quite often observed in what are thought to be, by unsuspecting church people, "fine Christian marriages" where the emphasis has been put on mechanical "roles" for each partner. These are thought to be "God's" roles, and personalities become twisted in trying to conform to these stereotypes. In such relationships there tends to be a strong dominance-dependence situation, because this is what many erroneously believe the Bible teaches.

Christians need to stand up and be whole people in Christ, receiving His revelation message into their innermost beings. It is important that they come to Christ for cleansing from guilt, so they can walk in Christ's righteousness as new creations, not constantly struggling under condemnation. Christian women need this balance in their lives, along with the proper humility and a gracious spirit. We must learn to perceive the difference between a haughty aggressiveness, which puts our husbands down and harms them, and the true dignity of a believer. Humility does *not* mean forever groveling in the dust. Love does *not* mean that we always have to be in the wrong. The believer loves himself (in Christ) as

Neither Male Nor Female in Christ Jesus

well as his neighbor; in fact, if he does not have a proper regard for himself, he *cannot* truly love and respect another. That is why the Word says, "Love thy neighbour *as thyself"* (Matt. 19:19) (and that means a lot!). It does not tell us to love others and hate ourselves. We hate sin in ourselves and others, but we can stand upright in Christ, cleansed from that sin, and respect and appreciate ourselves.

It seems that Christian women need to be told this. It frightens them, for they do not want to become "masculine," haughty, prideful, or boastful of their gifts. But the fact is that only a few are in that danger. Most are in danger of going to the opposite extreme of being too shy and retiring and too self-effacing (to the point of exhibiting mild masochistic behavior); thus, they bury their gifts. When they see what God wants them to be as women, some are terrified that this new light will break up their relationships with their husbands who do not yet understand this truth. So they let the truth slip through their fingers and return to bondage rather than risk upsetting their husbands.

What can we say in this situation? Remember that some men *need* to be shaken up at this point. Their male egos are too inflated, at the expense of their wives. And there is such a thing as a woman showing righteous indignation at times. Jesus certainly exercised it when it was suitable, and so did other servants of God.

Nevertheless, we must remember that the weapons of our warfare are spiritual, not carnal, and that in a difficult situation, a wife must often be prepared to move gradually, using prayer as her main weapon. She must never lose her love, proper humility, or graciousness in moving out into a fuller sphere of liberty. If possible, she should obtain advice from others who already know this freedom, rather than from those who are still in bondage on this particular point. A lot depends on the personality of the man. Some men really do have very fragile egos, which need building up. Others need to deflate theirs a little! And there are women of both types, too! We must not allow resentment to build up within us in such situations, but seek to have the mind of Christ at all times. At the same time, we must hold firmly to our freedom and refuse to move back into bondage, particularly in our spirits. It may sometimes be necessary to give way to tradition and custom for a time to keep the peace, but we must hold on at all costs to the liberty of the Spirit.

I have previously explained how God allows us to go through trials and how the gifts He has given us will eventually make way for themselves, provided we are trusting in God. But let us not be like yo-yos in our new-found freedom, forever vacillating, wondering whether bondage is the right way after all.

The Right Answer: Agape *Love*

Situations like the ones mentioned above call for *agape* love in our homes. Many family situations demand this kind of love in a special way, and the Christian woman will constantly be looking to God for the infusion of His love. I am confident that if a mother, wife, father, or husband truly perceives the wonder of this love, he or she will cry to the Lord for it to be manifested in the home. The woman or man who ministers this love exercises the highest kind of ministry.

Perhaps, dear sister, your husband does not treat you as he should. *Agape* love will help bring through the Lord's answer to your prayers. Perhaps he is not even a believer. Maybe you are one of those who suffer from a husband who drinks, curses, wastes the family income, and has no care for the things of God. The Bible exhorts you not to nag, but to pray and to exercise love. Remember, *agape* love never fails! But God may test and try your faith, and you must be prepared for this and ready to hold on in faith. It is by "faith and patience" that we inherit God's promises.

The only hindrance to our exercising God's love is selfishness, pride, or resentment in our own lives, or lack of faith. Remember, Christ died to himself—to His own rights and pleasures—in order to fulfill a greater purpose. He also died for us, and through identification in this, we too can die, when necessary, to our rights and pleasures in order to win our loved ones to Christ or to promote harmony in the home. We can do this without in any way losing our dignity. We do not have to become servile. We can just exercise when necessary the higher right of giving up some rights. This is quite different from masochism. The spirit of it is utterly different.

Christ's death was effective. It still is. It means we can enter into His power. By a miracle, His death is our death to sin and selfishness. As we appreciate His death, then His life can also be effective in us. We can enter into His riches. The secret is in our identification with Him by faith in His death, His resurrection, and His triumphant life.

By this identification I will be able, in the *right* spirit, to lay down my life and all it represents for my husband and my children. I must count myself as dead to my own wants, but alive to the needs of my children, grandchildren, and husband. We do not forget ourselves all the time, but there are times when this total self-giving is called for. To live in this self-giving spirit is possible because "I no longer live, but Christ lives in me."

When we come to this place, our hearts will pour out in torrents of unquenchable love for our families and for our spiritual families as well. We can pray and ask that the Lord take our blessings and give them to our loved ones. Our hearts may cry out for their complete redemption. We rise up in faith, count our prayers as already answered, and praise God. As we praise Him, a joy and expectancy wells up within us. We are putting *agape* love into action in our prayer life.

Oh, the wonderful privilege of the *agape* prayer life! It can be the greatest of ministries, exceeded by no other. If intercession is your *only* ministry, take heart! It is a wonderful one. Some who are sick or elderly, crippled or otherwise laid aside, cannot do very much else, but they can pray. If you are in this situation, give yourself in love to this ministry, and you will be amazed how God uses you!

PART THREE

Some Important Bible Terms

We have already looked at a few Greek and Hebrew terms in some depth, particularly the words translated "prophesy" and "prophetess." An understanding of such words in the original can help drive away prejudices, which are often based on inadequate English translations. We have seen, for example, that the Greek verb translated "to prophesy" means far more than that word usually connotates in our pentecostal churches. When we look at the role of the prophetesses, we find they often spoke in public and gave extended discourses, or sermons. There is no basis for the idea that a woman was never allowed to preach in public in biblical times. The many prophetesses readily prove that!

We also looked together at a few problem passages. In this section we will consider in detail a few more biblical terms. Like words in any language, those of the original biblical languages may vary their meanings according to context. Most words, in English as in Hebrew and Greek, have several meanings or shades of meaning. This is why it is difficult for a nonspecialist to identify with certainty the meanings of some biblical words in their particular contexts, and this is also why we have a number of different English versions of the Bible. A mere bit of knowledge of the original languages should not be too readily displayed! We do better to turn to the experts, remembering that even they may make mistakes or disagree.

Errors can be made by experts as well as laymen when they make their decisions without reference to God in prayer. Lack of revelation from God in studying a passage can lead to false conclusions. But this does not mean that revelation is a substitute, as some seem to think, for sound scholarship. Occasionally we hear ignorant Christians putting themselves above the scholars and claiming revelations contrary to sound scholarship. The truth is we need both. Not that we can all be scholars, but we can all use their work and respect it, while also looking to the Spirit for His revelation in His Word. The work of the scholars is part of the great heritage of the Church, and we should receive this work and use it humbly, not as if it were an infallible interpretation of the Word—for the scholars are fallible men, too—but with serious respect. Without the work of the scholars, we would not have the Bible in English at all!

Remember how in Galatians law and works put a veil over the hearts of the believers of Galatia, and deception resulted. They sought to mix law with grace and thus failed to heed God's revelation. Their whole understanding of the gospel was thrown out of focus. The role of women, too, has often been misunderstood because law was mixed with grace, and heed was not paid to both the scholars and revelation.

1
The Meaning of "Headship" (Kephale)

Ephesians 5:23 tells us the husband is the head of the wife, even as Christ is the head of the Church. *Kephale* (pronounced kef'-a-lay) is the usual Greek word for "head" and the one used here. It is used literally, to mean that part of the body we call our head, and also figuratively, in various ways. *Kephale,* used in this figurative manner, can mean high rank or the end of something. It can mean an extremity or the uppermost part of anything.

The word often means "origin," or "source," like the source of a river in mountain snows. Eve was drawn from Adam's side, so in a physical sense of origin, he is her source. Note that Eve was not drawn from Adam's head, to rule over him, nor from his feet, to be bossed about by him, but from his side, to be an equal partner in God's sight. Notice, too, that just as the mountain snows may be a source of water to the river, feeding it from its fresh snows, so Christ is the source of life, salvation, and blessing to His Church. This is one meaning of Christ's headship. In the same way, the husband is to be to his wife a source of blessing, encouragement, protection in need, and joy. He is to help her enter into freedom and break free in Christ from the curse. Furthermore, in a physical sense, his body is in a wonderful way the source of new life; through their love, a little child can grow in his mother's womb—surely one of the greatest miracles of creation. This is an often forgotten but wonderful meaning of the word "head," or "source."

Kephale also means "first." Christ was the first of the new creation, just as Adam (the name means "man") was the first human being of the old creation.

Two Possible Views

1. In reference to husbands and wives, this passage in Ephesians can be variously interpreted. Most commonly, it is believed that verse 23 is a *moral precept,* an eternal teaching about how Christian marriage should be. According to this view, the husband should be the head by virtue of a *spiritual status* God has given him.

2. Other learned commentators, however, believe differently. Dr. L.A. Starr, for example, in a very thorough study of all the references to women in the Bible, gives a different suggestion in *The Bible Status of Women* (Fleming H. Revell). She explains this verse as referring simply to the *legal status* of women and of husbands in the Roman Empire of that day. Paul always advises Christians to obey the laws of the land as far as possible, and, says Starr, he is simply using the unquestioned law of the day as an analogy with Christ's headship over the Church.

The Meaning of "Headship" (Kephale)

We have already mentioned the Roman law of *Patria Potestas,* which held sway in New Testament times. By this, the man was absolute head of the household, and his wife and children were his property with no rights of their own. He had the very power of life or death over them. Starr does not believe this headship of the husband is meant to be primarily spiritual, but is rather *simply a recognition of the actual legal status of all husbands of that day.* She does not believe it is intended to apply for all time. This commentator is a highly skilled student of the Bible and of the original tongues, so her opinion should be taken seriously.

Because this absolute law was in force, people had to obey it. Paul simply acknowledges this and tells the woman to accept this law, so the gospel is not blasphemed. He also lightens her burden far beyond the conception of any of the heathens of the day by giving a very demanding charge to husbands—"*love* your wives, even as Christ also loved the church" (verse 25). He knew that in those days women suffered under the burden of the Roman law. But he also knew their burden would not be hard to bear if their husbands loved them unselfishly, as Christ loved His Church! Her submission would then be willing and joyful, because she could utterly trust her loving husband.

Which interpretation is correct? Is this a spiritual and practical *command* for all time in all Christian marriages, or is it a statement confined to those days, one which, recognizing the law of the Roman Empire, seeks to lighten the woman's burden in relationship to that situation? It may well be the latter.

As we shall see later, there are *many* commands and practices in Scripture which we no longer follow today, because we believe they were meant for a particular society at a particular time. This does not mean we honor them any less as God's Word. We hold all of God's Word in the very highest esteem and do not follow some who, in pleading for women, ignore or reject parts of the Bible. Not at all! The question at hand is one of interpretation. All the Bible is God's Word, but some sections speak directly to all people in all times, while others speak particularly to certain long-past situations (though we can still profit and learn from these parts). These references to the husband's headship could well be primarily legal in nature. After all, the Bible says elsewhere that "there is no difference" between man and woman in God's sight. It lays firm foundations for growth in the Church over the centuries towards greater freedom for women, greater release from the curse.

View One: Marriage as a Subjection-Dominance Relationship

Let us suppose that the thrust of Ephesians 5 is in fact spiritual and practical, and is meant for all marriages past and present. (This is the view mentioned first in this chapter.) Let us assume that it does present an eternal principle. *This may not be the case,* but we will make the assumption and then try to discover what, in this case, "headship" would mean. We have already looked at the meaning of *hupotasso,* "to submit," as used in the passage. We have seen that it does not mean servility or servitude. And we have seen that men are also told to

The Meaning of "Headship" (Kephale)

submit—the same word—to other Christians, which would include their wives, in a general sense. So nothing can be required of the wife in submission that is not required of all believers to one another and, in a special sense, to God. What is the meaning of the husband's headship, if we take it as a permanent principle?

The word *kephale* does not mean "boss"! That is important to realize. The husband is not told to boss his wife around, any more than she is told to obey his every whim in an obsequious manner. We have mentioned one meaning—"source" or "origin"—which gives us a beautiful interpretation of headship.

Notice, too, that if we take this verse as a permanent principle, it does *not* mean that all men are heads over all women or that all women have to submit in a particular way to all men! We often find Christians acting as if this were the meaning. But it clearly says (Eph. 5:24) "let the wives be subject to *their own husbands*" and "the husband is the head *of the wife*" (not of everybody's wives, daughters, mothers, and aunts!).

We should see that the idea of "headship" is used in various ways in the Bible. Notice in particular:
1. Christ's headship position in relation to the Church
2. Christ's headship position in relation to Satan and evil
3. The husband's headship position in relation to the wife

1. Christ's Headship Over His Church
Christ woos His Bride to himself with His great love.

He leads and guides her in love. He protects and covers her and teaches her from His wisdom. Yet He does not boss His Church around. He is not a tyrant, and He does not force His will upon her. He wants us believers to love and honor Him as a matter of free will. He gives us lots of responsibility and freedom of choice. His headship builds up our individual personalities and never destroys them. Never does He trivialize or dehumanize us.

More than that, Christ as Head of His Church shares His righteousness and glory with us! We become identified with Him, and we share His throne rights. Someday we will reign with Him in glory! His is certainly not the headship of a dictator or of an army commander.

Christ's love is so great that He gave up His rights and came to earth as a baby, to grow up as a man and to die on a cross for our salvation. He humbles himself utterly, not standing on His dignity, though He might well have done so. He gave up all He had in His love for us, giving himself even to death. And instead of grasping to himself His absolute right to rule, He lovingly shares His throne with His Bride.

All through the Bible, even in the Old Testament prophecies, Christ is represented as a servant. He told us He came to minister (serve), not to be ministered unto. He could have commanded instant obedience; instead He comes to us as a humble servant! He tells us that the one who would become great should become like Him, the servant of others.

Love and servanthood, humility and self-giving—these are the key points of Christ's headship as expressed in

The Meaning of "Headship" (Kephale)

relation to His Church. What an inspiring picture!

2. *Christ's Headship Over Satan and the Powers of Evil*

How different from his headship to the Church is this expression of Christ's headship! He does not woo Satan by love, give himself as a servant to the powers of evil, or care for and protect them! Of course not! Hell has been prepared for the devil and his angels, for they are in total rebellion against God and cannot be redeemed.

In this relationship, Christ's headship takes on all its power, authority, and majesty. When He speaks a word against them, they shrivel. At Christ's return in glory, they will be utterly destroyed. Christ shares with us a degree of the authority of His headship over Satan. Through prayer and through speaking the word of faith, we can participate in routing the devil and his armies, but only in the name of Jesus. Such authority resides in His name, which is above every name. It does not reside personally in you or me or in our own names!

3. *The Husband's Headship of the Wife*

Which kind of headship is the model for the husband? If we are taking the Ephesians 5 passage as an eternal precept, it will be very important to answer this question. It is easy enough to answer. The husband's headship is likened not to Christ's headship over Satan but to His headship over the Church. But some Christian men seem to forget this. They lord it over their wives, selfishly demand their own way in everything, treat their wives as nothings and act like domineering masters—by divine right! They think that a little superficial loving now and then fulfills their obligation to love their wives! How far from the truth! No man has a mandate from God to act that way. How different is the Christian ideal from that legalistic institution called by some believers "the Christian family"!

Christ humbled himself. There was no room for selfish ego or male chauvinism. Love is the very essence of His headship towards the Church, and so it must be for the husband who follows this model. Notice, too, that the analogy is imperfect and incomplete. Only in some ways can the husband be like Christ. The comparison can only be partial, for men are not Christ! They are not God, not the Savior, and not infallible!

If Jesus makes the Church joint heir with himself, the husband will share his rights and privileges with his wife, too. As Christ made himself a servant to His Bride for love's sake, so the husband will do the same. He is to love her as Christ loved the Church, never taking advantage of his position, and being willing even to give his life for her if need be. A loving husband does not *demand* submission to his headship, even as Christ does not. The wife gives this respect and love willingly as the husband shows a Christlike spirit towards her. This is *agape* love in operation.

We are reminded of the great love of Hosea, a type of Christ in the Old Testament, for his wife, who had deserted him and been unfaithful to him, who had even debased herself to the extent of becoming a prostitute! Yet he bought her back and loved her. That is true *agape*

The Meaning of "Headship" (Kephale)

love operating in the most impossible circumstances. Christ believed in the power of this love to win the Church's love and submission. The husband loves his wife the same way.

Notice how the Church is seen by Christ. She is His Bride, His Body, His army of the Cross and His ambassador corps. She shares His throne (cf. Eph. 6:11-20; 2 Cor. 5:19-21; Eph. 1:19-23; 2:4-7; 2 Tim. 2:11-13; Col. 1:13-23). His Church has authority over the powers of Satan in His name (Col. 2:15), and when His people ask anything in His name, He does this for them (John 15:16). Christ sees His Church as a powerful, glorious, and reigning Church (Eph. 1:17-23; Col. 1:13-22). And the Church feels keenly her need of Christ, of His protection. She confers with Him and acts in the light of His victory.

As a wife with a good husband, sharing in his glories and feeling her need of him, has good reason to honor him, so the Church has good reason to honor and surrender to her King and Savior. It is not to an undeserving Christ that the Church bows her knees. At the same time that she humbly bows her knees to Him with love and honor and adoration, she also remembers that she is seated alongside Him (Eph. 2:6) as His ambassador (2 Cor. 5:20) and a queen (Rev. 1:5-6). He has made us to be joint heirs with Him (Rom. 8:17), to share His authority and His glory, to rule and reign with Him (Col. 2:9-15; Phil. 2:9; 1 John 4:4). How beautiful is this true picture of Christ and His Bride (Rom. 6:3-11; 8:28-39; Rev. 21:2-3; 22:17; Heb. 8:6-13). If we take this picture (as Paul suggests we do) in relation to the husband being the head of the wife, we see the complete picture of headship. (Of course, as we have said, the picture does not fit the home *all* the way. The husband is not Christ and not infallible!) Following is a summary of the husband as the head of the wife:

1. The wife is to recognize her husband as the head and confer with him in all major decisions. She is to respect, honor, adore, and yield. She is not to undermine him, be domineering, bossy, or pushy, or be selfish or filled with pride. She is to be acting as the Church does toward Christ.
2. The husband is to earn the right to have this position by serving his wife and through his love, unselfishness, and humility even laying his life down for her if need be, as Christ did for the Church.
3. The wife should act on behalf of her husband's interests and for his honor and glory and good (as the Church does for Christ's honor).
4. The husband is to consider his wife equal with himself, sharing his position (as Christ did with the Church—Romans 8:17). He is to be a source of joy for her.
5. The wife is to be considerate, understanding, appreciative (as the Church is to Christ).
6. The husband is to protect, care for, and love his wife (this is the *agape* principle).

Ephesians 5:24 says, "Therefore as the church is subject unto Christ [in the same manner and for the same reasons], so let the wives be to their own husbands in every thing." "Every thing" in this instance is conditional.

The Meaning of "Headship" (Kephale)

If the husband is fulfilling his part—or, as one commentary states, whenever the husband is subject to Christ in everything—the wife is obligated to be subject to him in everything; but if he is *not* subject to Christ in everything, the wife is *not* bound to her husband in everything. If she has a husband who is not walking in the truth, and she desires to win him to Christ's truth, then elsewhere Paul gives certain instructions as to how to go about winning him. If he cannot be won, does not appreciate her Christlike life, and desires to be free from it all, the wife is not bound to her husband (1 Cor. 7:15). She is *never* expected to disobey God to please her husband!

"Husbands, love *(agape)* your wives, even as Christ also loved the church, and gave himself for it; That He might sanctify and cleanse it with the washing of water by the word, That he might present it to himself a glorious church, not having spot, or wrinkle, or any such thing; but that it should be holy and without blemish" (Eph. 5:25-27).

After Christ died for the Church and gave His life for it, He rose again from the dead to present a glorious bride to himself. First, the Church responded to Christ's death when He laid down His life for her. She accepted His sacrifice. She believed in Him because she had seen the great love with which He loved her. Second, His death resulted in her redemption. He raised her up and seated her beside Him, giving her His authority and allowing her to share His throne. He cleansed her by His word. Third, she believed His word. Therefore, it was by faith and grace that she became a glorious Church, not by law, or words, or demands, or unbelief, or fear. Christ never demanded a thing, but wooed His Church until she began to see His headship to her.

Ephesians 5:28: "So ought men to love their wives as their own bodies. He that loveth his wife loveth himself." So it is with men; they are to love their wives as Christ did and does love the Church, which is His Body. No man has a right to *demand* that his wife recognize his headship, because Christ is responsible for this. But if a husband will do what Christ has done, then his position will be recognized by his wife.

No wife has the right to withhold recognition of her husband's headship if he is submitted to Christ. If he is not submitted to Christ, then she can try the great and wonderful *agape* love to win him to a place of submission to Christ. Paul declares that this will never fail.

"For no man ever yet hated his own flesh; but nourisheth and cherisheth it, even as the Lord the church" (verse 29). See the tenderness and care and understanding of Christ to His Church! This same tenderness and care and understanding applies to husbands and wives. Actually, the husband and wife are a type of Christ and His Bride, in every respect:

1. The husband lays down his life for his wife.
2. He redeems her from the curse through Christ.
3. He serves her in love, as Christ serves His Bride.
4. He is a source to her of new life, love, joy, protection in times of need, even as Christ is the source of these things to His Church.

The Meaning of "Headship" (Kephale)

5. He seats his wife beside him in authority and shares with her his name, his status, and his rule. Remember that the Bible, in 1 Timothy 5:14, actually tells the wife to *rule* the home with authority; the Authorized Version says "guide the house," but this is far too mild a translation. The Greek word is the one from which we derive our word "despot." It means to rule with strong authority, as mistress of the home. The wife is thus entitled to rule the home with her husband, and he is to share his authority with her, if he is following the example of Christ in His glorious headship.

The Scripture does not allow a husband in any way to suppress a ministry God has given to his wife. Nor does it suggest she is to be a timid, passive, or helpless creature. That is quite a false picture of femininity. The wife and mother in Proverbs 31 is a good example of true femininity. In the same way, the Church is not supposed to suppress its ministries or to be weak, timid, and passive.

Christ's headship in no way means that His Bride has to be made up of people of one kind of personality—timid and passive—in order to be submissive. Where has the false idea come from that women, in order to be submissive, must all have weak, passive personalities? That is the opposite of God's will. Some women use this false idea of the "Christian woman" to hide from reality and responsibility. This is not God's intention.

The Church is made up of many different personalities. Wives are very different, too. Some are naturally more shy and retiring than others. Some are very outgoing, efficient, and businesslike. All can be truly God-fearing women. It is wrong to criticize the outgoing woman, to label her "aggressive" or suggest she is unfeminine just because she does not fit into the false stereotype. How dull the world would be if we were all the same!

The modern woman needs probably less protection than women in earlier times. But there are occasions when she may be vulnerable to some kind of attack or violence, and then her husband can lovingly protect her, because of his greater physical strength. It is often dangerous, for example, for women to walk out on the streets at night. This is where the husband can give his protection and care. And when she is ill, expecting a child or caring for small children, she needs his care and protection in a special way, too. (Just between us women, there are some of us who feel out of sorts at certain times of the month. A hint to make you and your family happier if this is your problem is to take several calcium tablets for a couple of days before and during this time. It usually does wonders to remove pain and to help you feel better, especially if you take a little vitamin D [too much is dangerous] with it, to help the assimilation of the calcium. Your body lacks calcium and often iron at these times. This is a good hint to pass on to your daughters. It is much better than taking heavy doses of aspirin.)

Incidentally, much nonsense is talked about concerning the effects of a woman's natural life cycle on her personality. We do have our "up days" and our "down days," it is true, but the average woman is not normally greatly affected either way. Arguments about women falling into

The Meaning of "Headship" (Kephale)

frequent states of depression or becoming semi-invalids at regular intervals are generally quite unfounded, and are sometimes used to prevent women from receiving appointments to responsible jobs, and so on. This is very wrong. The truth is that doctors know men also have hormonal and mood cycles, that they have "up days" as well as "down days," too. And there are many men who are more moody than women. It depends on the individual rather than on your sex.

Another very interesting fact, recently discovered, is that two people who live close to each other, such as man and wife, tend naturally to flow together psychologically in their mood cycles. As they adapt to each other, their cycles adjust to each other! A number of experiments have shown this. They have also shown, unfortunately, that some drugs, such as contraceptive pills, can often disrupt this natural adjustment of the cycles to each other, resulting in some disruption in the home. It is helpful to know these things and to be understanding of one another.

Just as we have our "down" days, so do our husbands. If they enjoy greater physical strength, women frequently have greater natural endurance than men, live longer, and have greater mental and spiritual strength (notice how many more women attend churches than men overall!). We are built to complement each other and to help each other out in times of need. We can give much to our husbands, just as they can give much to us.

To follow Christ's example of headship means that the husband does not take all responsibility away from his wife. He does not make all the decisions himself and insist on his own way. He takes an interest in her life, and she in his. He shares as much as possible with her of his job and business world, and if she happens to be a woman not very familiar with things like banking, insurance shares, etc., he helps her learn about these things rather than treating them as a mystery or using them to prove his "superiority." After all, plenty of women deal with such matters every day. Every wife needs to learn. If her husband dies and leaves her to manage the family alone, how will she handle important business affairs; how will she be able to recognize potential problems?

Some husbands think their headship entitles them to handle all the finances, but there is no biblical ground for this. The woman in Proverbs 31 handled plenty of finances herself! Nor is there any biblical reason whatever to suppose that headship means making all decisions, always having the last word, always being the one to take initiative. These concepts are the mere traditions of men.

Overall, I think we can see that the command to husbands to love their wives as Christ loved the Church is a more demanding one than that which asks wives to respect and defer ("submit") to their husbands!

View Two: Marriage as Partnership

If we take "headship" in Ephesians to refer to a timeless principle of Christian marriage, we should remember the real meaning of Christ's headship to His Church. This type of headship is not oppressive. It liberates rather than enslaves.

The Meaning of "Headship" (Kephale)

But we must not forget the other, very possible, interpretation of that passage—that it is simply an analogy, a comparison based on the actual legal situation of those times, not binding on all marriages everywhere for all time. We make this allowance for the times in our interpretation of many other elements of Scripture (see our later discussion in this book of some of these).

If this is the case, it means that other passages, such as Galatians 3:28, are to be seen as more basic principles— God created us equal and has redeemed us from the consequences of the curse. Therefore the Church is working towards equality and towards a greater freedom for women than the male headship of Roman times allowed. If this is the correct interpretation, most of the attitudes we have suggested above will still be correct, of course. Husbands will still be expected to be loyal, loving, and protective when this is needed. They will still need to exercise that self-giving *agape* love. But more responsibility for the same kind of love and loyalty will be placed on the wife also. And "submit yourselves one to another" will be thought of as a more basic principle than "wives, submit yourselves to your husbands." The relationship will be more a two-way affair, and a very beautiful and fulfilling relationship will result.

Many, many Christians today accept this or a similar interpretation of the Scriptures. Their marriages are *partnerships* in a fuller way than ever was possible in Roman times. Neither tries to dominate the other. Decisions are made together. The husband is strong enough in his spirit and secure enough in his manhood that he has no need to stress the idea of headship, nor to feel dominant over a dependent wife. He loves her so deeply he wants her to be fully herself, to grow and blossom in her gifts and ministries. Far from being threatened when she achieves and is successful, he rejoices with her. And in the same way, the wife realizes she can no longer hide behind her husband from the real world as a passive, dependent being. She knows she would not develop a full personality if she were to make no decisions and wait on her husband's word for every action. That is a child's life, not a responsible adult life. She moves out as a unique person and soon is strong enough not to feel threatened, either, if her husband does better than she does at something. She rejoices at his success and ministry and supports him fully in all. In return, she receives his full support. And neither is she afraid to be herself if she has a greater ministry than he. She does not flaunt such a ministry or make him feel small, of course, any more than he does this to her. But if she has a greater ministry than he (which often happens), she knows it is God who has given her this gift, and that she must exercise it. Both of them are secure enough in being themselves. Neither has to pretend to be less than he or she really is to protect the other's ego. They simply exercise what God has given them in humility, love, and faith, and each partner builds up the other one.

This is important, because our tradition suggests that the man should always be more prominent, more successful in work or ministry, than his wife. If she is more successful or better known, people may tease the husband.

The Meaning of "Headship" (Kephale)

How cruel! How damaging to both! It often happens that a woman marries a man who does not have as many gifts as she. But tradition says that his ego must be protected at all costs, even if she has to pretend all her life to be dumb, or give up opportunities for service! But if the opposite situation arises, and the husband is clearly more gifted, no one worries about the deflation of his wife's ego! Why is his pride and ego so much more fragile and important than hers? True *agape* love protects both men and women from humiliation as neither partner deliberately tries to outdo the other or to pridefully vaunt his or her gifts. Rather, each includes the other, builds up the other, and lives humbly. Each is secure enough in being just what he or she is, without the need to feel superior or to force the other to downgrade herself so he can imagine he is superior!

Even in school, girls are often told to hide their good grades lest the boys decide they don't like them! They are told not to answer too many questions in class, as this would turn off potential boyfriends. And so, at a very young age, they are often encouraged to hide their gifts and talents under a bushel in order to "get their man." Surely that kind of man is hardly worth "getting"! Yet millions of talented and gifted women spend their lives hiding their gifts or allowing them to atrophy because they fear that their husbands might feel inferior! This is questioning God's wisdom in creation! If women always had to be inferior and men's pride always had to be pampered, God would have made all women less gifted and less intelligent than all men. Then we could simply have accepted the situation as natural. But, in fact, God made us *individuals* who happen to be male or female. Some individuals are highly talented and some are not, just as some are beautiful and some are not. Some have ministry gifts and some have ordinary gifts of the Spirit. No research has ever shown men as a whole to be more gifted than women. Intelligence, like spiritual gifts, is evenly distributed between both sexes. But we women have been much slower to use what we have. We have often done just what Jesus told us not to do in the parable—we have buried our talents in the ground!

In a real partnership marriage, *both* partners exercise their gifts to the fullest, each fully supporting and encouraging the other, and neither boasting. Much of the time they work together in *team ministry*, so that neither one outshines the other.

Those who believe that a partnership view of marriage is permitted by Scripture for today, in contrast to the headship concept of the Roman times, are often under attack. The most common objection is that "every organization must have a head and a leader; otherwise chaos will result." This of course is untrue. What *is* true is that every organization needs headships and leadership, but not necessarily "*a* leader." Christian partnership marriages do have a Head—Jesus himself! And they certainly have leadership. Both parents lead and direct the family together, because they take seriously both the leadership role of the husband *and* that of the wife (cf. the proper translation of 1 Timothy 5:14—"let the wife *rule* the home with strong authority"; it is hard to account for this

The Meaning of "Headship" (Kephale)

verse if we take the husband's absolute headship as valid for all time). There is authority and leadership, but not authoritarianism or one-man rule. The marriage is based on equality rather than on dominance-dependence.

Many families that are run this way are much happier than those run according to what many suppose to be the "biblical" way. Often the children are less rebellious, too. This is another argument in favor of the partnership interpretation of Scripture, as over against the absolute-headship-of-the-man interpretation.

But whatever we conclude, we cannot use the argument that every organization must have *a* leader. When we look around, that is just not true. More organizations in our society are run by partnerships of some kind than are run by one man. Business partners share authority and decision making. Sharefarmers work together. Companies have boards of directors and voting shareholders. Schools have school boards and school councils. Governments have upper and lower houses and elected representatives. Experience has shown that government is more fair when more people participate in it. Countries governed by one man or even by one party (without an opposition party) are usually petty tyrannies. We see again and again that ultimate power should not be in the hands of one person. The same thing, many Christians believe, is true on a small scale in the home.

But, say the critics, what happens when there is a stalemate? Surely you need a head to make the final decision. But business partnerships do not work that way. If two mature businessmen are partners and cannot agree about something, one of them gives way, or they come to a compromise. Or perhaps they decide to do nothing for a time and then think it through again. They certainly do not decide beforehand that Mr. Jones will always have the final word in any disagreement, for that would be grossly unfair to Mr. Smith. Christian partners in a home can seek the mind of the Lord together and usually come to agreement if they are walking close to Him and are mature people, not always wanting their own way.

Partnership may mean a few more difficulties in reaching decisions than if the man always does the deciding. But those in partnership believe it is worth that extra little inconvenience to incorporate the two partners as full participants in decision making. The process itself helps them grow and mature and understand each other. Partners like this believe that a deep *friendship* between two people is basic to marriage, and that friendships are not based on prior decisions about who will always automatically have the last word. True friendship, they feel, would be threatened or destroyed if one of them was to say, "We are building a friendship. We're going to do a lot of things together, so someone will have to be the leader. Otherwise we will not be able to make decisions and our friendship will be chaotic. So I will be the leader." They feel this is what the old kind of so-called "Christian marriage" does, and that it spoils their relationship by making them unequal. They believe that the man's headship was completely appropriate in biblical times, under Roman law, but that this is no longer the case. They believe God's Word carries in it the seeds of a greater

The Meaning of "Headship" (Kephale)

freedom in marriage, of greater equality for both partners. And often their happy Christian homes bear out their interpretation.

Your Decision

I am not going to make the decision for you. I leave you to decide which interpretation of Ephesians 5 and related passages you accept. Both are held by sincere, Spirit-filled believers.

You may decide that a partnership marriage is God's ideal for today, and that the basic principles in the Bible demonstrate this, even though the husband's headship was stressed, as it probably had to be, in New Testament times. Husbands then were to follow the law of the land, and so were wives. But the law today is quite different. It often seems as if the Church is lagging behind in needed reforms, instead of leading the way. It seems to many that the secular world is giving wives greater freedom from the curse than is the Church—how odd! Those who hold this viewpoint believe they are following the true spirit of Scripture rather than the letter of the law and are moving into the fullness of Christ's redemption.

Marriage, you may decide, is no longer to be based on the old Roman law of *Patria Potestas,* the background against which the letter to the Ephesians was written. God is speaking to us afresh in new situations and telling us to adapt to the new laws of our land and the new and legitimate freedoms, just as He told people to adapt to the law and the restrictions of their day. (Of course, we are referring here to proper freedoms. We are not suggesting that anyone should give in to immorality, etc., just because some modern people do so!)

On the other hand, you may decide that the traditional interpretation of Ephesians 5 is the right one. The husband is meant to be the head of his home for all time. It is an eternal principle. (Many Christians teach this, of course, and it may be very hard for us to break away from this interpretation.) If we make this decision, we must look in detail at the meanings of words like "headship" and "submission," to make sure we are following God's will. (Recall the earlier discussion.)

It is your choice. But either way, as a woman, you can enter into liberty. We cannot be certain which is the right interpretation, but in neither case did God intend you to be weak, dependent, and passive, or to be bossed around. In neither case, we have shown, does God intend the husband to be the "boss," make all the decisions, do all the ruling in the home, or always have his own way.

So, dear sister, your marriage can move into liberty. Try to help your husband see these things, too, and pray for him. Love him with all your heart. God is bringing you out of the curse and into the glorious liberty of the children of God!

2

The Meaning of "Submission" (Hupotasso)

We have already looked briefly at this Greek word, so we will not give a lot more space to it here. But it is closely connected in Ephesians 5 with "headship."

Hupotasso really reminds us of the principle of *agape* love more than that of dominance and subjection. It means to place ourselves beneath someone else, or in other words, to honor others above ourselves—"preferring one another in love." It means to honor and respect someone, to defer to another. And in some contexts it means to subject or subordinate to someone or something.

Like the word for headship, the word for submission is used differently in different places. When we speak of the powers of evil, Satan and his angels being subjected to Christ's power, we mean that they are finally forced to obey Him. They are far beneath Him and are His enemies. When we speak of the submission of believers to Christ, we speak of something very different. It is a willing, loving, and joyous submission to our Lord, who we know wills only the best for us. He is far greater than we, and we feel that it is right that we give Him first and highest place and honor Him.

When the Bible speaks of people submitting to each other, the meaning differs from both of the above situations. But in spirit, the meaning is closer to the submission of the believers to Christ. It is not totally the same, however, because in God's sight, one person is not higher than another person, in the way that God is above us, or Christ is above the devil. There is not the same gap between those submitting and those to whom they submit. God is no respecter of person. Also, among people, submission is not absolute. It is never forced the way Satan is forced to be subject to Jesus. It is given willingly and lovingly, more the way the believers submit to Christ.

Furthermore, because people are not as mighty as Christ, nor are they infallible, submission is not absolute and therefore does not involve so much the idea of obedience without question as the thought of putting the other's well-being above our own, honoring and feeling reverence for the other, seeking his or her interests before our own. It means that we defer to others—seek their advice, consider their wishes, consult with them.

In short, if we are exercising *agape* love, we are submitting to the one we love in many ways.

Some constantly stress that wives should submit to their husbands (Eph. 5:22, 24), but they say little about verse 21, which stresses that *all of us* should submit to one another in the fear of God. Submission to one another is part of the normal loving behavior of the people of

The Meaning of "Submission" (Hupotasso)

God. One famous exegete reminds us that this means that while wives are to submit to their husbands in a *particular* way, husbands are to submit to their wives in a *general* way. The submission is not all one way! This is implied in submitting to one another—husbands too will find themselves submitting to their wives if they obey this precept. (This point was brought out in a sermon by John Stott.)

Notice too that the passage never tells women to submit in a *particular* way to *all men,* but to their own husbands only! Some churchmen forget this. The general command in verse 21 applies equally to men and women and in both directions. Again, it is not a legalistic principle, but the exercise of love.

Since the word used in verses 21, 22 and 24 is the same in each case *(hupotasso), the husband cannot demand from his wife anything more than the general body of believers can demand of one another by way of submission.* Whatever *hupotasso* means in the one case, it means in the other. There will be more opportunity and need in the home for this submission than in the ordinary life of the Church, because husband and wife live more closely together. But the kind of submission referred to will be of the same kind in each case.

Rightly speaking, the husband does not *demand* submission in any case, for it then loses its essential quality of self-giving love. Submission is something we *give,* not something we *take.* The husband who takes verse 21 as seriously as the rest of the chapter knows there are many occasions when he also gives submission to his wife, out of love.

WOMEN IN MINISTRY TODAY

Naturally, how far we take the idea of the wife's submission to the husband will depend upon how we interpret headship for today, for submission in marriage is in some ways the other side of headship. Those who believe a correct interpretation leads them to a partnership marriage rather than one built around male headship will still see the real need for loving submission in marriage, but they will put more stress on *mutual* submission (one to the other) in love, as in verse 21, and less on submission seen as the *duty* of the wife to a divinely constituted head, her husband.

In any case, biblical submission is not to be seen as servility. It is a giving of self in love to another, and the Bible clearly teaches that we are *all* to practice it towards one another, and not merely wives to husbands. Submission to one's husband as a duty may have been enjoined because of the Roman law of the times, which made the husband legal head of the home. Therefore it may not be a command of eternal and abiding importance; it may not be very relevant to us today. You can make your own decision about this. The need of all believers, however, including husband and wife, to submit *to one another* is a quality of love which is timeless in its implications. This we cannot avoid, and do not wish to avoid. It did not depend on the Roman law but is an abiding principle.

Whichever view of Ephesians 5 we take, submission *to each other* plays an important role in marriage, as it does in church life. In both views, submission of each to the other is required and it is important that husbands remember that verse 21 indicates that they too must be

The Meaning of "Submission" (Hupotasso)

ready to submit to their wives, for the command is general and refers to both men and women.

The Jesus Style in Relationships

An interesting new book, *Women, Men and the Bible*, by Virginia Mollenkott, shows clearly the biblical teaching about how Christians are to relate to each other.

The Jesus style in human relationships is always *mutual submission*. Before Paul specifically asks wives to submit to their husbands, he gives a general command to all believers: ". . . submit yourselves to one another because of your reverence for Christ" (Eph. 5:21, NIV). That means all of us. It does not exclude husbands, either! Paul then goes on to explain how this mutual submission is worked out. One way it is worked out is for wives to submit to their husbands. Another way is for husbands to love their wives "as Christ loved the church." And so on. Because Paul has just said that we are all to submit to one another, it is hard to see how we can interpret the next part of the passage to mean that wives only are to submit and husbands are to dominate.

Mollenkott shows that we have made too big a difference in this passage between "love" and "submit." We have thought that these were quite different roles. In fact, when we think about it, and read the passage in its context, we realize that the two belong together. Submission involves love, and love involves submission. Paul is not saying that wifely subjection excludes the wife from loving her husband. And neither is he saying that husbandly loving excludes the husband from submitting to his wife, from often deferring to her wishes instead of always selfishly insisting on his own way and his own "rights."

Indeed, if the husband is to follow the example of Jesus in loving his wife, this certainly includes taking a servant role—a submissive role—as one part of that loving. The husband is to follow Christ in emptying himself for love of his wife, not in puffing himself up with pride and refusing to consider her wishes! See Philippians 2:3-8. Here again, Paul talks about the Jesus style in relationships. Take time to reread this wonderful passage.

The Jesus style is that everyone loves and serves everyone else, submits to them and defers to their wishes. And in particular, the strong are to *serve* the weak, not domineer over them.

The *carnal* way of relating in the Bible is dominance-subjection. Yet many Christians assume this is the Jesus way! Christlike submission and humility have been taught only to women, and husbands have been encouraged to believe that they should dominate, make all the decisions, and expect their wives to be the ones to make all the sacrifices! What a cruel parody of the Jesus style! Often, too, wives are cajoled into manipulating their husbands surreptitiously from behind the scenes, because they have been denied their proper say in the family. How dishonest! How ultimately damaging to true communication!

In the carnal way of relating, it is easy for the dominant one to become filled with pride. Have you ever noticed that in many Christian families which are run according to this traditional dominance-subjection model, the wives tend to be childish? Or they have little personality and

The Meaning of "Submission" (Hupotasso)

their lives seem very dull and predictable. They are not as mature as other women. This is one of the tragic results of a carnal way of relating, which has been dignified, quite falsely, as "God's plan for couples."

Normal people grow by responsible decision making, but the wife in a carnal relationship is stunted in her moral and spiritual growth because she is never able to make important decisions. She is kept in a perpetual childhood; it may be a happy childhood or an unhappy one, but either way, it is still childhood. She lives vicariously through her husband and children. She is deprived of a rich and direct personal relationship with God. She simply accepts her husband's will as God's will. He accepts all the real moral responsibility. Yet strangely, the marriage books tell her that she is nearly always to blame if anything goes wrong with the marriage! If her husband is interested in another woman, it is probably because *she* isn't pretty enough or attentive enough. If they are unhappy, it is because *she* isn't submitting enough. And so on. And all the while, the husband is encouraged to please no one but himself! Though lip service is always given to the idea of him loving his wife, this is rarely given much true biblical content.

Submission, then, should characterize *all* Christians, not just wives. It is really the opposite of self-assertion. It is the desire to get along with each other, not insisting on one's own status and rights. It is the desire to serve another in love. *Love* and *submission* are really just two sides of the same coin; they amount to nearly the same thing. And they are enjoined on *all* believers. Let us work for the Jesus style in human relationships, including marriage!

3
Other Terms

You will remember from the earlier discussion that the word translated "usurp authority" in 1 Timothy 2:12 in fact merely means "exercise authority." Paul is saying it is wrong for a woman to exercise authority *of her own accord* over the men. No one in fact should do this. When we teach, we teach with Christ's authority, not our own. And we do it because the eldership of the assembly or others in authority have invited us to do so. We do not impose our own authority or push in when uninvited. Also, husbands may well ask their wives to minister with them or to take their place. Where permission is given or a request has been made, no private authority is being exercised, and there is no usurping of power.

We remember too that women's position in those days was by law so much lower than today that the Church had to be careful not to harm the witness of the gospel by allowing women to rush in to public ministries that might be too controversial. Often they were associated with street women if they did certain things. Hence the greater restrictions on women's ministries. We would not expect such restrictions today, because the social situation has completely changed. The gospel is much more likely to be harmed and the Church spoken ill of if they fail to give to women at least as much freedom in service and ministry as the world gives them!

We remember too that the word *hesuchia* is sometimes translated "silence" when it refers to women, but differently when it refers to men. Such translators were unfortunately using "unequal balances" and allowing their traditional prejudices to affect their scholarship. (The same is true of the translation of 1 Timothy 5:14—"let the women *guide* the house." It appears that these male translators just could not face the true implications of the Greek, "let her rule the household with power and authority.")

First Timothy 2:12 tells the woman to "be in silence" (Authorized Version). In fact, the Greek adjures her simply to be "quiet" (cf. the New English Bible translation, and other versions) or "at rest, at ease." There is a difference between quietness (not disturbing the proceedings or trying to take over without permission) and absolute silence!

We also looked at the meaning of the words "to teach" (and in fact there are several such words). Some passages appear to forbid women to teach. We saw that there were particular forms of teaching, especially the public office of teacher, which involved disputes in the streets and synagogues, which would have been very bad for the wit-

Other Terms

ness of the Church at that time had women taken these on themselves. Paul's concern, and that of others at the time, was mainly for public order and a good witness to the outside world.

We know that women cannot be forbidden to teach on all occasions and forever, as a permanent principle, because if this were true the Bible would contradict itself. After all, Paul also taught that there was no difference between man and woman in the things of God. The gifts of the Spirit are given both to men and women; there is absolutely no suggestion that some ministry gifts are given to men only. If God gave women gifts they were not supposed to use, that would be very odd! It would mean that women with teaching gifts had to hide their talents, just the way Jesus told us *not* to do!

Furthermore, we know of a number of Bible women who *did* teach and who were commended for their ministries. There is no doubt at all that women may teach other women and children. Already, that gives us two-thirds of humanity whom we can teach (Titus 2:4; 2 Tim. 1:5, etc.)! But more than that, Priscilla taught Apollos (even though her husband was with her, she still taught, and did not sit by in silence), and she later became widely known for her ministry, which must have been to men as well as to women. Huldah, in the Old Testament, very probably taught young men in the school of the prophets. And the many women whose names are mentioned as co-workers and deaconesses (the word really means the same as that used for the men, "deacons") also must have done some teaching in groups that included men.

WOMEN IN MINISTRY TODAY

We have established beyond doubt that many women in the Bible were prophetesses, and that the verb translated "to prophesy," among its various meanings, definitely has the central meaning of speaking out in public, and of giving an extended sermon. Thus no one can say women are forbidden to preach. These women prophesied in public, in the open and in big assemblies where men were often present.

It is very hard to know where preaching and prophesying ends and teaching begins. In preaching and prophesying, it is hard not to do some teaching at the same time. The two ministries overlap so much. In the same way, when giving counsel to others, it is hard to avoid some teaching. Huldah unveiled the future of the nation. When the lost book of the law was found, it was she, rather than Jeremiah, who was consulted, and her word was accepted as God's word. Surely there is some teaching involved in this, too (cf. 2 Kings 22 and 2 Chron. 34).

Deborah too must have done some teaching in her ministry. She was a wife, but she was also judge of all her nation and a prophetess of great fame. Her gift made way for her and she must have sat often before the Israelites, pouring out to them God's wisdom and instruction, and declaring His whole counsels (cf. the article on Deborah in H. Lockyer's book *All the Women of the Bible*, Zondervan).

Deborah was also an agitator. She stirred up public discussion to try to change the low spiritual condition of Israel. She aroused the nation, as day after day she excited those who gathered to hear her. She was a warrior, and

Other Terms

after leading her people to victory, she ruled fairly over the land for forty years. As well as all this she was a poetess and, if not an actual mother (we do not know), certainly a spiritual mother to her people. In all these tasks Deborah often took the lead, exercised great authority, commanded men as well as women, and taught the things of God.

For these and many more reasons, we know that Paul's comments about not permitting women to teach were not intended to be blanket prohibitions for all time and all occasions. He could hardly have meant to contradict the rest of Scripture. Nor could he be saying that our liberty under the New Covenant is less than under the Old Covenant (which had a place for women like Deborah, Huldah, and Miriam). Our position today must be at least as good as that of Old Testament women. Anything they could do, we can do if God gives us those particular gifts and callings. Even if there were only a few women who did those things, the meaning is still clear. God does not forbid it. If He did, it would *always* be wrong, and there would be *no* exceptions like Deborah. And such women would be criticized and punished by God. But instead, they were honored. (Miriam's punishment was *not* because she was a woman who had become "uppity," as some seem to think!) Naturally, there were not many women in Bible times free to exercise such ministries, for those were the days before contraceptives, and women usually had large families to care for. God is practical about these matters! But women today often have greater freedom and smaller families, as well as greater control over their own reproductive processes. This means we are freer to fulfill God's will for our lives in the use of our gifts.

Why then did Paul say women should not teach? As we said before, the only reasonable answer is that he was forbidding certain kinds of teaching, which at that time were unseemly. The great concern was for the good name of the Church. Their testimony must not be spoiled by upsetting more than absolutely necessary the customs of the day. People already told lies about the young Church and were critical of it. They said Christians were atheists and cannibals! Possible converts were frightened off. Paul could not have people saying they were immoral as well, and that their women acted in improper ways, according to the traditions of that time and place.

The Real Point: A Good Witness

What do we learn from this? Not that all women should be forbidden to teach and that many other legalistic forms should be carried over to our times. Rather, we learn a principle—that the Church should adapt as far as reasonable to the customs and laws of the particular time and place, in order to avoid offending people unnecessarily. The Church's actions should help people see the Church and the gospel in the best light possible, so they will not be turned away.

What is turning away many unbelievers from the Church today? Not women teaching, but the fact that many churches do *not* allow women to play their full role in the government and ministry of the church! Some

Other Terms

thoughtful atheist or agnostic women (not extremists) say, "Why should I join the Church? I have more freedom as a woman among atheists than among Christians!" Others say, "The Church does not treat me as a full human being, but only as a second-class citizen. It wants to turn my marriage into an unequal relationship, whereas at present I enjoy a wonderful equal partnership with my husband, and we are very happy. It refuses to allow me to preach, teach, or do anything worthwhile in the Church. Why should I become a Christian? It would take me backwards a hundred years!"

Again, one hears comments like these, "In ordinary society, I am fully accepted by non-Christians. I am a specialist in my profession. I lecture in a big college. I give public addresses and present papers at international conferences. Men and women alike come to hear me, and I go to hear them. We accept each other fully as people and not according to rigid sex roles. It never occurs to the men in my audiences to refuse to listen to me because I am a woman! But when I go to church, there and only there I am a victim of discrimination and prejudice! I am not permitted to speak in front of even a handful of men. I find this treatment insulting and ridiculous. I have no time for the church anymore."

Such comments are frequently heard. Women say they can do more useful work in community service clubs than they can in the Church. They complain that non-Christians accept them and give them important responsibilities and invite them to address big meetings. But at church they are just expected to bring the flowers and make the tea. That is "women's ministry." Some women say, "If God really feels that way about half the race He created, I am not sure that I want to know Him!" They complain that unbelievers are more understanding and treat them in a more respectful, kind, and appreciative manner than Christians do. Ordinary, less educated women often feel the same way. And so do countless non-Christian men. They too are turned away by the Church's usual attitude toward women.

Many Christians who walk in greater freedom are turned away from the charismatic movement by some extremists who put women down and make many restrictive rules against their ministry. They see certain popular charismatic books on women and on the so-called "Christian family" and are shocked at the legalistic, patronizing attitudes to wives which these books reveal. So they turn right away from the movement and lose the opportunity to enter into the fullness of the Spirit. They simply do not want to be part of a movement where the men are likely to put them down so much. The rather sugary language of paternalistic books and sermons does not prevent them from tasting the bitter pill underneath, and they are revolted.

This is the sad truth. We are not talking only about extreme "women's libbers." We are talking about thousands of good, ordinary women and men, many of them highly educated and thoughtful people, who honestly cannot wish to turn to a God whom they see enshrined in the traditions of prejudice in the churches. This is one of the major factors *today* which is turning people away and

Other Terms

spoiling our gospel witness. It is virtually the *opposite* situation from that in Paul's day.

Should we not look again at our traditions? We will find many of them to be only "traditions of men," old prejudices not really taught in the Bible at all, and dishonoring to God. We cannot, of course, ever alter basic gospel truths and doctrines, but the Bible itself shows us how to adapt many aspects of our *practice* to the customs of the day. There are big differences between the practices of God's people in the Old Testament culture and the adaptations to God's people in the New Testament culture. Many of the changes in emphasis and practice we see between the two Testaments were not changes between the two *covenants* at all. The changes in the covenants were essentially changes in the administration of the gospel itself. But most of the other changes between the two Testaments were changes made to adapt to the very different *culture* and customs of the Roman Empire. The times were completely different from the days of the ancient Hebrews in Palestine.

And the same way, today, when missionaries take the gospel to new cultures, they preserve the essentials of the message, but alter many other things to fit the culture. They adapt to the local situation, because this is what we see done in the Bible itself. This is the very principle of Incarnation, to make the Word of God meaningful in a particular human situation. Jesus first did this by leaving His heavenly glory and coming to earth as a human being and living among us. A completely heavenly gospel, with no relation to ordinary people or to our life on earth,

WOMEN IN MINISTRY TODAY

would be unintelligible to us. When we fit the container of the message to the culture, we are really just doing what Jesus himself first did.

Of course it is not always easy to tell whether some matters are an essential part of the gospel and unchangeable, or whether they should be adapted to the situation. That is why we left you to make your own decision about the headship of the husband and the particular submission of the wife. But we need to think very carefully about some of our inherited ideas and customs concerning women's role and ministry, for these things are causing great harm to our witness today, just as women who dressed like "prostitutes" or taught men may have caused great harm to the witness of the Church long ago.

Often through history the Church has led important movements of social reform. But far too often, she has been the *last* to see the need for changed attitudes and reform. In the Middle Ages you were in danger of being burned at the stake if you taught that the earth was round, or that it traveled round the sun. Many Christians supported the slave trade until other Christians helped lead antislavery reforms.

More often than we realize, we cling to traditional interpretations and ideas—mainly because we have never thought much about them or because some preacher or church we admire teaches that way. We feel sure we are following God's Word, but sometimes we are just following the accumulated prejudices of past generations. We become so conservative in everything that we hardly dare to "think change." We imagine that the stereotyped roles set down for women and men in our society and church are really related to our inborn nature and to God's laws, when much of the time, neither of these is the case. And the prophets of doom come to warn us that if we change the role of women at all, children will be neglected, families will fall apart, and our society will collapse! They do not see the difference between extremist chaos and wise change in line with the deeper teachings of the Word.

PART FOUR
Questions and Answers

1
Basic Questions

To test our understanding, let's pause awhile now. Can you give some answer to the following questions yourself? Try, and then compare your own answer with the one given.

Question 1: *What did God say about women in the first part of the book of Genesis? What law were people under in that age?*
Answer 1:
   A. God spoke to man and woman together in the Garden of Eden. He told them to be fruitful and multiply, to replenish the earth and to subdue its vast resources. He told them to have dominion over the fish, birds, and animals (Gen. 1:28-31). Both man and woman were to participate in reproduction and in child care; both man and woman were to work and to build civilization. Notice that God did *not* give them two separate roles: women to be

concerned with child care and men with building civilization and culture. Both were given both commands. They were to work together as a team.
B. Woman reigned with man in the natural and spiritual realm. She governed with the man. She was equal with him (Gen. 2:18, 22-24).
C. The law they were under was the personal rule of God.
D. Then, after Eve and Adam had sinned, God put upon Adam the curse: "By the sweat of your brow you will eat your food," and thorns came to trouble him, weeds to increase his work (Gen. 3:18-19, NIV). His curse was not the work but the hard *toil* of work. Otherwise work would have been a joy. And God spoke again to Eve, this time with a curse: "I will greatly increase your pains in childbearing; with pain you will give birth to children. Your desire will be for your husband, and he will [begin to] rule over you" (verse 16, NIV). (Note that our studies in the Hebrew showed that this was the *first time* man ruled over woman; it was a curse, not a creation ordinance!) Everything was upset by the Fall, even the natural world. Eve lost her queenly position. She no longer ruled with her husband in the same way; she lost her personal responsibility as well as her governmental power, to a large degree. Man was a slave to himself and woman a slave to the man because of sin.

Question 2: *What did God say concerning women in the*

Basic Questions

days of Moses? Under what law were the Hebrews of that time?
Answer 2:
  A. God made temporary provision for women to find redemption (looking forward ultimately to the cross of Christ). They could make sacrifices, attend feasts, and take vows. (See Deuteronomy 12:11-18 and Leviticus 27.)
  B. Women were used by God as prophetesses (Exod. 15:20; Judg. 4:4; 2 Kings 22:14; 2 Chron. 34:22). Women were still under the curse as were men, but God wanted them to begin to follow Him again and to find a way to be free of the curse. Certain people were released more fully than others from the curse because of their faith and obedience. These included Abraham, women like Sarah and Miriam, and later Huldah and Deborah.
  C. They were under the Law of Moses and especially the Ten Commandments at that time.

Question 3: *What do we read about women in the books of the prophets, and in Psalms and Proverbs? Under what law did people live at this time?*
Answer 3:
  A. We will find many encouraging things said about women right through the Bible, if we seek them out. Among the prophets, Joel spoke particularly of the great outpouring of the Holy Spirit which would come upon women as well as men. It would be an anointing for the purposes of preaching and

WOMEN IN MINISTRY TODAY

of ministering in God's authority (Joel 2:28-32). The fulfillment began at Pentecost, and we are experiencing further fulfillment of this wonderful promise in the charismatic outpouring of our own day.

B. The book of Proverbs has much to say, but we particularly remember the description of the ideal wife and mother in chapter 31. We need to continually refer back to this chapter to correct the views of many Christians today who see women as weak, dependent and homebound creatures.

C. About this time, the children of Israel and Judah were carried into captivity. They were ruled by one heathen empire after another and so came under various laws. But they sought to maintain for themselves at least the religious and ceremonial laws of Moses and the book of Leviticus. Women were often poorly treated throughout this period.

D. These books make no mention of the subjection of women or the headship of men.

Question 4: *What did Jesus say about women? Under what law did the people live during Jesus' day?*
Answer 4:

A. Jesus never put down women at all and never spoke to them of subjection. He always treated them well and talked to them even when they belonged to another race. This was very unusual. Jewish men did not normally talk to women at all in public. There is no hint in any of the Gospels that Jesus

Basic Questions

relegated women to an inferior position. Some say that He never chose any women as His apostles and that this shows women should not be preachers or evangelists. But in fact there *were* a number of women who often moved about with the apostles and shared with them in ministry (Matt. 27:55; Luke 24:22). And there were women apostles later in the early Church, including probably Junia (Rom. 16:7). It is perfectly natural that a single man in those days would not choose women to be among the original twelve apostles, for either these women would have to leave their husbands and children to follow Him, or they would have to be single women (of whom there were very few). In the latter case, the team would have certainly been accused of immorality. How could single men and women travel and live together like this for so long without arousing suspicion? And how could wives leave their families without occasioning criticism? But it seems likely that some of the apostles took their wives with them; presumably they did not have small children at home.

To the woman caught in adultery, Jesus said, "Neither do I condemn thee: go, and sin no more" (John 8:11).

To the woman who pushed through the crowd to touch Jesus' garment for her healing, He said, "Thy faith has made thee whole" (Matt. 9:22).

To the mother who begged healing for her daughter, Jesus said, "Great is thy faith: be it done unto thee even as thou wilt" (Matt. 15:28).

To Mary of Bethany, who anointed His feet with fragrant ointments and wiped them with her hair, Jesus said, "Wherever the gospel is preached, this act of love shall be remembered" (Mark 14:9, paraphrased).

To Martha of Bethany, who fussed about the house with domestic matters while her sister sat at Jesus' feet and learned, He said, "Martha, don't worry so much about cooking and serving; it is the spiritual things which are most important. Your sister has chosen the better part" (Luke 10:41, paraphrased). And ever since, people have been telling Christian women that housework and domestic duties are their *main* calling, and that this work must come before all else—quite different to what Jesus said! (Of course we should see things in perspective; this is not an injunction to neglect our homes and families, either!)

B. Jesus gave some wonderful promises to his disciples. He prayed in John 17 that all his future disciples would grasp those promises (John 17:20). So here are some of the things He said to us women:

He told us all that whatever we ask in His name, He will do it for us (John 14:14).

He said all his disciples would do *greater works than He had done* in His name after He had gone (John 14:12). Such is women's ministry!

Jesus included women when he said, "Behold, I give you authority over all the power of the enemy. . . .

Basic Questions

In my name you will cast out devils, heal the sick, and speak in tongues" (from Luke 10:19; Mark 16:17-18, paraphrased).

C. In Jesus' time Palestine had come under the dominance of Rome. As a Roman colony they had to obey Roman laws. Some of these were good laws, but many, such as the law of *Patria Potestas,* were bad and unenlightened. Women's position in these times was low, as it has so often been through history, because of the curse.

D. As we have seen, Jesus never put women down. He never talked about the headship of the man and the subjection of the woman in marriage. He gave much teaching about conduct and attitudes, but never mentioned any differences between the ministries of men and women. His promises were to *all* believers. He never said that women could not hold offices or positions of authority.

Question 5: *What did Jesus say about women at Calvary? What did His death achieve for women?*
Answer 5:

A. At Calvary, Jesus said to women, in effect, "I have paid the price for your sins, just as I have for men. You are now free from the curse and from the penalty of sin. Rejoice and enter into your freedom! You are cleansed and redeemed. You have passed from death to life. You are a new creation." Through the childbearing (when Mary bore Jesus) the Savior had come into the world. Woman had played her part in the Fall, and now a woman played her part in redemption. Now women can be free, at least to a high degree, from the penalty of sin and the curse, and walk in newness of life (cf. Gen. 2:16; 1 Tim. 2:15; Rom. 5:12-15; and so on).

B. Jesus also showed women that they could now be seated in heavenly places with Him and reign with Him, just the same way that men could, if they believed in Him. Women also have a place of authority and share the rule of God. How then can the husband fail to share *his* authority with his wife, when Christ has shared with her His own authority and power?!

C. Jesus says to women that Christ has redeemed us from *all* of sin and *all* of the Fall. He is the second Adam. While we may not experience the completeness of that redemption until His return, we can enter right now into much of it. Woman is not left to endure the penalty of sin and the effects of the curse now that Jesus has come. Woe to those legalistic Christians who try to tell her that her curse is irredeemable! Is that not a blasphemy?

D. No Scripture referring to Calvary suggests that women cannot be redeemed from their curse. No Scripture referring to Calvary talks about women's subjection or man's headship. In the victory of Calvary, woman's great Head, as man's, is Christ himself.

Question 6: *What does the book of Acts say about*

Basic Questions

women? Under what law did people live at that time?
Answer 6:
- A. The Acts of the Apostles tells us that the Holy Spirit was poured out on all the believers. In the upper room on the day of Pentecost, many women, including Mary the mother of Jesus, prayed together, were filled with the Spirit together, and spoke in other tongues. They were imbued with the power of the Spirit to be His witnesses (Acts 1 and 2). They were to use this power to witness and to preach, as well as to live for the Lord.
- B. Acts tells us about the four prophetesses, daughters of Philip the evangelist. Paul and his party stayed at Philip's house. These daughters were preaching God's Word in public and speaking forth in the inspiration of the Spirit. Paul did not rebuke them and tell them that women had to be silent! He evidently quite approved of their ministry (Acts 21:8-10).
- C. Acts warns us of what happened to a woman who lied and tried to deceive the Holy Ghost. She died for her sin, as did her husband for his (Acts 5:8-10).
- D. Acts never mentions woman's submission or man's headship. At no time are women put down. Many of them ministered in different ways in the early Church.
- E. These people still lived under Roman law, as they did throughout the New Testament period, including the time about which the Epistles were written.

WOMEN IN MINISTRY TODAY

Question 7: *What do the Epistles say about women?*
Answer 7:
  A. Paul mentions many women who worked with him in spreading the gospel and one who was probably a lady apostle (Junia is a feminine name) (Rom. 16:1-23). The deacon Phebe is commended, and so is Priscilla. Her name is listed before that of her husband, something unusual in that day, because she had a remarkable ministry. It appears from Church history that she later went to Rome with her husband and ministered to the fugitive church which had to meet in the catacombs under the city. Her name is carved there as "Prisca."

Paul also mentions Mary, who bestowed much labor upon him, probably both in the practical and spiritual realms. Tryphena and Tryphosa were some kind of female ministers, too (verse 12), and history suggests they were church leaders. Elsewhere (Phil. 4:2-3) Paul mentions Euodias and Syntyche, who held leadership positions but unfortunately were quarreling about something (as plenty of men leaders also do, sad to say). He asks them to be of one mind and work as a team.

Paul actually mentions a considerable number of women whom he regards as his "co-laborers," the same term he uses for men who worked with him. It is unjust to conclude that all these women did was cook and sew for the men workers; no doubt they helped in these practical ways, but they clearly had wider ministries in the spiritual sphere as well.

Basic Questions

Paul also talks about women in some of the passages we have previously studied together. We will not repeat this material here except to say that *Paul is the only writer in the Bible who talks about women's submission and men's headship, or who suggests that there are times when he doesn't like to let a woman teach.* He also told women to dress modestly and simply, as good witnesses to the gospel.

Does Paul's stand mean that Christ took the curse of poverty, the curse of everlasting death, the curse of law and the curse of backbreaking work from man, but decided to leave upon woman her curse, to have pain and trouble in childbearing and to be dominated by men? "Paul," we may say, "you puzzle us. No other Bible writer seems to say these things."

But as we have seen, Paul is not contradicting the rest of Scripture. He is fitting in with the customs of his time and of his day, so the gospel witness is protected from slander. And, if we are wise, we will take his lead and do the same today, fitting in as far as is possible with the customs and culture of our own time, so that evil will no longer be spoken of the gospel, and so that unbelievers will not criticize our poor treatment of women. While basic principles of good living and basic doctrines remain unchanged, the *outworking* of the principles and the doctrines will often differ according to time and place.

We can always benefit by others' experience, by knowledge of their laws and customs, and so we can still benefit from those parts of the Bible which no longer apply to our society. We can draw out the golden thread of basic principles and truths, woven through the whole fabric. And we can apply these same principles in new ways to our own situation. Christianity is essentially a faith of living relationship. It is a charismatic faith which speaks to us today. It is not a religious system of rigid rules and regulations, though there are always new Galatians wishing to make it so!

2

Further Questions for Thought and Reflection

Question 1: *If we insist that Paul's instructions to women in his day should be followed exactly as they stand today, shouldn't we also insist that* everything *in our churches be run just as it was in Bible times?*
Answer 1: In some ways this would be a good idea! Women would have some ministration in every meeting, as they did in Paul's time, for there were many more different gifts exercised than usually are evident in our modern services. Also, as the women sat on one side of the church and men on the other, the women always administered the Lord's Supper to their own sex. Women always laid hands on sick women when prayer was requested. And outside of church time, women visited and counseled women. After all, it was considered morally wrong for men to go anywhere near women. Of course, to do things as they did in those days, in every detail, would inconvenience us a lot, too. But if we say that every detail must be followed, then we can neglect nothing!

WOMEN IN MINISTRY TODAY

Our big church buildings would have to close, and we would meet in homes or perhaps in Jewish synagogues! We would wash one another's feet and greet each other with a holy kiss. Organs, pews, hymnbooks, pulpits, ministers' robes, stained-glass windows, even lighting and heating such as we have today, would be outlawed.

Communion services would be proper meals. We would not have Sunday schools or youth services and fellowships. There would be no church schools, no gyms or football teams, no church offices or secretaries.

The minister would probably be a part-time worker, unpaid, or paid just a little, with no theological training. He would probably be one of our number, from our own town, and not sent to us by "headquarters." His main task would be to mobilize our different ministries and get us using our gifts. He would not be expected to run the services as a sort of one-man band, the way it so often happens today. That at least would be an improvement! We would come closer to the priesthood of all believers than we are at present!

Women would wear veils rather than hats. We would not celebrate Christmas or Easter. Indeed, we would not even use the New Testament in our services, just the Old, and we might read it in Hebrew or in the Greek Septuagint translation.

We would exhort Christians to take a little wine for their stomachs. And there would be many other changes. Would you still feel at home in a church like that, or would you prefer to leave it and join another denomination? But then, of course, if we followed the New

Further Questions for Thought and Reflection

Testament pattern across the board, in all our churches, there would be no denominations!

In India, and in some countries we have visited, churches are still run rather like that, for their customs, which have changed little over the centuries, were originally quite similar to those of the Middle East.

Question 2: *If we insist on following some of Paul's instructions to husbands and wives of his day in detail, shouldn't we try to follow them in every detail? And if the society that gave rise to those commands was right in its treatment of women, shouldn't we try to work for a society more like the Roman one?*

Answer 2: We know that Paul's basic teachings about love and mutual respect and submission in marriage are principles valid for all time. No problems there. But what about the details of marriage and family life? If we insist on the husband's headship as an eternal principle, and the wife's subjection as well, could it also be that other matters should be considered eternal, too?

Christian girls of that time could not choose their own husbands. Would it be better if parents still chose partners for their children? The young man who was attracted to a Christian girl would first have to approach the head of the household—her father. If he said no, that was the end of the matter. But the daughter could also be married off by her all-powerful father to someone, maybe a rich but ugly old man, against her will. Fathers were paid a bride price for their daughters, so a rich husband was an attraction to them.

Girls were strictly chaperoned, so we would have to follow suit. They could rarely go out in public alone, and then only with long heavy clothing and veils. This might help prevent immorality.

If we wanted to reproduce the situation in New Testament times, the father would be head of his family with a vengeance! He would own his wife and children like property and they would have no rights at all. If his wife committed a crime, however, *he* would be brought to trial! The wife did only her husband's bidding; she was considered a child with no responsibility for her own actions. The husband could have his family put to death if he wished. They were his property, so no one would object. Yes, the husband was really boss in those days! Should the churches lobby for laws like this today? Or at least introduce such practices in their churches? In many countries there are still laws like this.

Wives would always wear veils. Some Christians today insist on women having long hair and wearing hats in church. To be consistent, they should insist on veils rather than hats, and require their wives to wear them whenever they go out. And they should allow their wives to pray and prophesy and speak or give a sermon in church—wearing their veils of course—because Paul said that veils should be worn when praying and prophesying in public.

These veils would be a sign of modesty. (They did not represent submission to men, contrary to what many believe.) You can still see veils in many Muslim countries. Some, like the *chadris* of Afghanistan, cover most of the

Further Questions for Thought and Reflection

face, leaving only a small fabric grille to look out. It is rather hard to recognize even your best friend in a *chadri,* but then women rarely go out walking anyway, and especially not alone. One writer has called the *chadris* "living tombs."

Question 3: *If we insist on the subjection of women as a biblical principle, should we not also think about reintroducing slavery? Or at least, should we not accept it in principle?*
Answer 3: The subjection of the slave to the master is as thoroughly biblical as the subjection of the woman to her husband. If we were to follow biblical customs in every detail, we could not condemn slavery! The New Testament assumes that slavery is as normal a part of society as the low status of women in that day. Never does the Bible condemn the institution of slavery, just as it never condemns the law of *Patria Potestas.* It tries to make the lot of the slave better by insisting that Christian masters treat their slaves well. And it seeks to make woman's position better by talking about mutual submission and by insisting that the husband love his wife as Christ loved the Church. Those changes greatly helped women and slaves. But they did not challenge or alter the legal position of the slave or the women; both were possessions of another person by law. Onesimus was told to return to his master, who evidently still is thought to have the right to own him, though Paul lovingly writes to Philemon to treat him well and receive him as himself, perhaps hoping he might set him free. And the wife is

still told to submit to her husband in everything, as if he has a right to expect this. Often the discussion of wives' attitudes to husbands and slaves' attitudes to masters comes in the same chapter. The two are linked.

You see, it never would have occurred to Paul to challenge the basic *institution* of slavery, or the legal *institution* of marriage in his day. Paul knew God's will was to obey the laws of society where possible, although he sought to instill in Christians a new spirit within that law. Of course, if he had had a choice, Paul would have preferred a different system, for, contrary to God's viewpoint, both Roman marriage and Roman slavery meant that some people were *owned* by other people, condemned forever to be second-class citizens without power, money, resources, or responsibility of their own. Why? Simply because they were born either slaves or women!

The early Church did a great deal to ease the ill effects of these evil systems on their people. Christian teaching meant *great social advance* for wives and for slaves at that time. But today, to follow the same injunctions would be *social retrogression,* because our laws no longer permit slavery at all and recognize women as people with equal rights in marriage and, increasingly, in other spheres of life.

The Church in the Middle Ages owned slaves. Women were treated badly for hundreds of years in Christendom, often as badly as in pagan religions. Now at last we are emerging from that. The seeds of this wider freedom were in the gospel all the time, and we were meant to

Further Questions for Thought and Reflection

discover them. There are basic principles of human dignity in God's Word. Man and woman were both made in the image of God. There is no difference between people based on race, color or social status. Are we willing to follow these wonderful liberating principles to their logical conclusion, or will we continue to try to restore a way of life which contradicts those basic principles?

The Word of God, we believe, is a seedbed of liberty for people of both sexes and of all races and colors, educated or not, rich or poor. Paul was inspired to record those principles, even though he was unable at that time to see their full implications for the future. He simply had to work them out for his churches as best he could in the legal and social situation of his day.

At Calvary, Christ broke the bonds of such inhuman systems. Our world will not reach perfection till the return of Christ in glory; we know that. Hence sin, the results of the curse, the old grave clothes of those resurrected to liberty, will continue to hang on for a long time, especially in non-Christian cultures that still have many oppressive laws. But the Kingdom is with us now nonetheless, and the grand movement of God's plan is inexorably towards greater liberty under God, towards realization of every human being's full potential, without the ignominity of being owned by someone else. In the old times, woman had no real chance to become a full person. Because she always had to obey her father as a child and then her husband as an adult, she never grew to true adulthood in mind and spirit.

True maturity is only possible when we have to make

many decisions for ourselves and take responsibility for our own actions. Without this, even our consciences are not free, and we remain immature and, in a real way, less than human. Such, too, though in much more hardship, was the fate of the slave. Women often lived in comfort, even in love, and yet remained dolls, children stunted in their normal growth, slaves in spirit. And some want to take us back to that in the name of Christianity!

Agape love, of course, denies all forms of slavery whenever possible. It demands we give the other person his or her freedom, just as one who loves a little bird wants to let it go free from its tiny cage to experience what being a bird really is.

Of course it is sadly true that some women, loosened from the bondage of their homes and husbands under the old laws, have abused the privilege. Some have fallen into sin and immorality, or have become hard, cold, and promiscuous, a tragedy of lost womanhood. They do not realize that they are taking themselves into a new kind of bondage, away from true human dignity and the steadfast love of a good man. But freedom always involves risk. God, in one sense of the word, took a great risk when He gave man and woman free will. As our children grow older, we give them more and more freedom. We pray for them and trust that as they go out at night, or move out into the hard world to live their own lives, they will remember all we have taught them. We take a risk. We know that we have to do this. Sometimes they betray our confidence, but that is simply the price of freedom and of true humanity.

Further Questions for Thought and Reflection

We should notice that God did not reveal everything to His children at once. He revealed His plan slowly, over many centuries, through many events and many writers. He showed people as much as they could cope with at the time, in the context of their own society. Thus Old Testament believers had far less revelation than we enjoy today. God did not condemn them for having several wives. He allowed arranged marriages, and the strange case of Leah and Rachel. Men without children were allowed to seek an heir by their maidservants, surely a practice Christians would consider abhorrent today!

The Old Testament, especially in Leviticus and Deuteronomy, is full of commands, many of which were not abrogated with the New Covenant. But we do not follow these laws today. And in the same way we do not follow every instruction in the New Testament. Not all fit our situation. We have to interpret Scripture wisely, to decide which are fundamental truths and principles and which are relevant only to a particular day and age.

The Gospels contain further revelation beyond that in the Old Testament, the Epistles give us more, and Revelation points us to the future. We still need the whole of God's Word, but we must see each section in its cultural and historical context. And although the canon of Scripture is closed, God has not stopped revealing himself to us—every charismatic believer knows this! Principles implicit in the Old Testament become explicit in the New. And principles implicit in the New Testament become more explicit in the continuing life of the Church.

WOMEN IN MINISTRY TODAY

Question 4: *If we believe women should never pastor, preach, or lead, should we not be consistent in opposing all women who do any of these things in any circumstances?*
Answer 4: Some are consistent in this, but they are very few. We would refuse, if we were thoroughly consistent, to attend any meetings where women played a leading role, lest the Lord punish us for collaboration! However good the woman speaker is, however much God seems to be using her, we must conclude that her ministry can only bring trouble.

We would prevent women from teaching Sunday school, except to very young children, and we would probably have to set an age limit, as a few legalistic churches do. She certainly could not teach older boys. No doubt the Sunday schools of our land would be in dire straits or fold up altogether without woman teachers, but we could comfort ourselves with the thought that Sunday schools are not really biblical either! We could not use women in youth groups, and if they were really to be "silent" in church, they would not be permitted to pray, prophesy, speak in tongues, interpret, or perhaps even give a testimony or sing.

We would not allow women to write for Christian magazines, as that might be a form of teaching. In fact, we might refuse to listen to women taking a leading role in secular affairs, because it is important to stand up for the truth as a witness to the heathen! We would switch off women speakers on radio or television and avoid college classes taught by women.

It would be embarrassing for us to observe all the

Further Questions for Thought and Reflection

competent women who today serve as prime ministers, members of parliament, senators, mayoresses, ambassadors, pastors, lawyers and queens. We would say that, competent or not, they were breaking God's laws. We would try to forget great lady missionaries of the past, the women leaders in the early charismatic movement, great women like Evangeline Booth of the Salvation Army, and all the others. We would also choose to forget about women leaders in the Old Testament and fob them off as "exceptions" or "part of the Old Covenant."

But now and again, we might wonder in our heart of hearts why God had so much prejudice against women, and why He gave them gifts which He then forbade them to use.

We would criticize lady preachers and others who have been leaders in their fields by saying they were "unfeminine" and "aggressive." We would crush and discourage every female ministry we encountered.

Question 5: *If we really believe that we must obey our husbands at all times, why don't we call them "lord" as Sarah did? Why don't we set aside our troublesome gifts and become thoroughly dependent on our husbands?*
Answer 5: We would virtually have to pretend our husbands were infallible. At least, this would make unquestioning obedience easier! An exaggeration, you say? Of course it is! Yet the truth is that many Christian wives and husbands interpret the Bible more or less like this. It is really the logical conclusion of many of the chauvinist ideas currently popular in our churches. Also,

the logical conclusion is that woman is more stupid and less competent and gifted than man. She is thought to be more easily deceived than man, because Eve was deceived. But common observation does not bear out these conclusions. Some women are stupid, others intelligent, and men are just the same.

Women often appear incompetent and dependent because they have been trained to be that way! It is pure myth that women are more moody, more illogical, more emotional and intuitive than men.

Wives who are totally dependent are placed in a terrible position if their husbands die, become ill, or desert them. They have no idea how to handle business or money, make decisions, or cope with life. They have no way of earning an income. It is utterly cruel to allow adult women to remain in such a state of ignorance and dependence at any time. If they are left alone, as many are, it becomes a tragedy.

Totally dependent women often believe initially that this is what their husbands want. They act as shy, passive, dependent creatures to win a man. Many young men also believe this is the kind of woman they want, the supposedly "ideal" Christian wife. Later, these wives often find to their dismay that their husbands lose interest in them because of their weak and dull personalities. Many times husbands later come secretly to dislike, even despise, a dependent woman. One often sees this happen. They may sometimes turn their eyes towards other women with more interesting lives and more assertive, adult personalities. That teaching which turns

Further Questions for Thought and Reflection

Christian women into nothings is a desperately sad one and a complete denial of the gospel of abundant life!

Such doctrines also do untold harm to the husbands. Often one sees domineering Christian husbands, puffed up with pride and male ego. They certainly have not understood the meaning of "headship" in the New Testament! While the wife is working to build up the husband's inflated ego at the cost of her own personality, the Lord has been trying to whittle him down to size a bit!

Some say, "Ah, but this cannot happen if the husband really loves his wife." That may be true, but if the wife takes an abnormally low place, she inevitably pushes her husband into an abnormally high place. Things get out of balance. It is bad for anyone to have his or her own way too much of the time!

The man who makes all the decisions, takes all the initiative, handles all the finances (perhaps except groceries), and so on, is really getting his own way too much of the time. Even if he willingly does what his wife wants now and again, it is often only in matters of unimportance. Some men love their wives, but this love does not extend to *agape* love. So their concessions to their wives are patronizing. They do not consider it their *duty* to share the housework if the wife is also working long hours; rather they feel she should be grateful when they choose to help her a little with "her" work. Such men know they can always call on their supposed "divine right" to have the last word if they want to. They assume that "hubby is always wiser," and this leads away from true team work.

PART FIVE

Women in the West Today

1
A History of Struggle

Since we no longer live under the restrictions of Roman law, women today, at least in the Western nations, are free to involve themselves more in the affairs of society. They still have quite a long way to go to achieve complete equality in pay, employment, business, and law, but very significant advances have been made. It took us a long struggle to obtain our own rights in marriage, property rights, and the vote. Reformers worked long and hard to save women from being treated like animals in the mines and factories, just as they worked to save young children from the same fate. We need to be grateful for these advances. It is not so long since, in British law, children, madmen, and women were all classified together as not responsible for their own actions!

Some knowledge of the history of the struggle for fair treatment for women is important for us all; we tend to take for granted most of our freedoms. American women (and others too) would find it enlightening to read a book like Eleanor Flexner's *Century of Struggle,* which tells the moving history of the women's rights movement in the United States over the last few centuries. It is quite unfair to suppose that all these women were extremists and "nasty, aggressive types." They were mostly women with a deep sense of justice and humanity. It is fashionable today to giggle about the suffragettes who won us the right to vote. Yet those women fought hard for a right we all take for granted. Often one is moved to tears in reading the history of women's struggle to be recognized as full persons.

Another excellent book to read, written by Joan and Kenneth Macksey, is *The Guinness Guide to Feminine Achievements.* (You can order the books mentioned from your nearest good bookstore. See Bibliography.) Guinness books are famous for their records of human achievement. Here is a book for your teenage daughters to peruse. They will learn the many wonderful things accomplished by women throughout history, often despite enormous odds. It is not written by extremists, but by a husband-wife team who simply wanted to find out what women have done through the ages. They include the "baddies" as well as the "goodies." I quote from the blurb on the dust jacket:

> A picture of quite astonishing success emerges, and on a scale which is often overlooked by those who regard women as the downtrodden sex. At the same time a feeling that women have for long been subject to devious and restrictive practices becomes quite inescapable in a book which, nevertheless, pays scant attention to extremist points of view.

A History of Struggle

Kenneth Macksey freely admits that his eyes were opened in writing this book with his wife. Joan Macksey, a mother of two children, while cooperating with her husband in this venture, maintained just the right amount of independence in writing on those subjects in which she is more knowledgeable. So the book is itself a good example of how a husband and wife can work together.

The book tries to counteract a strange omission in most of history. When we read traditional history books, we find that women have been almost entirely left out! They only appear in obvious roles like queens, mistresses of famous men, or in a few other cases. In Australia, some studies of high-school textbooks showed that there were periods of as long as one thousand years that were treated without one mention of a woman! Could it really be that in an entire millennium there was not a single woman who did anything memorable? No wonder our daughters settle for passive roles and low expectations! No wonder so many girls become conditioned to believe that there are very few kinds of work open to them, that high aspirations are "out" for women!

But these days, one of the good things that is happening is that people are defining "history" more broadly than ever before. Once "history" was mainly wars, politics, plots, and intrigues. Perhaps it is to our credit that females were left out of a lot of that! Now historians realize that, really, "history" is "whatever happened in the past." Social history is becoming popular. People are interested in how ordinary people lived in days gone by. They write histories of trade, histories of costume, histories of toys, histories of the lives of children. They study the history of transport, housing, cooking, and leisure time. And what an interesting subject history then becomes!

As soon as we define history more broadly, women come into more prominence. They did lots of interesting and important things. They were inventors, writers, musicians, novelists, doctors, educators, and so on. Often they were resisted and trodden down by men. They were overprotected from the harsh world if they were well-to-do. A "lady" last century did not walk past a butcher's shop lest her delicacy be offended by the sight of all that raw meat! But they were underprotected from exploitation if they were poor. In both ways, they were prevented from being full human beings.

Women in Missions

In Christian service, too, women have made tremendous contributions. Far more missionaries have been women than men. Many have gone, with their husbands or alone, to remote and very dangerous places to carry the gospel. Miss Young founded the South Sea Evangelical Mission. Mrs. Long founded the Aborigines Inland Mission.

Women doctors went to the Middle East to care for sick women who otherwise would have died of their illnesses or in childbirth because custom did not permit them to see a man doctor. Women gave their lives serving God in hard climates before there were vaccinations available against tropical diseases. Many lost children in such places. There were some mission fields which were called

A History of Struggle

"the white man's grave," because nearly all who went to serve there eventually caught malaria or some other then-untreatable tropical disease, and died. But as some died, others came in their place—brave men and brave wives and courageous single women.

But even in missions, women had to battle to gain permission from churchmen to serve their Lord as He had called them. You may find it enlightening and inspiring to read the history of women in missions, *All Loves Excelling* by the famous American church historian Dr. R. Pierce Beaver. Again, it is often enough to make one weep, while rejoicing at the strength and perseverance of our sisters.

Before 1800, mission societies were all-male. Then Miss Mary Webb gathered together fourteen Baptist and Congregational women and started the Boston Female Society for Missionary Purposes. They did not yet go out as missionaries. They gave money to missions and they prayed. But progress was slow. Unbelievably, male prejudice was so strong that churchmen even opposed this. They did not approve of these godly women meeting together for prayer and giving to missions!

Later it was gradually accepted that women could raise money for missions. They still do a lot of this work today. But mission boards did not want to give them any place in decision making. Many missions today still refuse to allow any woman to serve on policy making committees, even when these women have served on the field faithfully for years. Young men, fresh to the field, are often preferred to women of long and outstanding service and experience.

WOMEN IN MINISTRY TODAY

And at home, the women who raised many of the funds for church and mission were denied any say in how that money was to be used.

For many years, no mission boards would send women overseas. Then, cautiously, they allowed a few wives to accompany their husbands. There was still no place for dedicated single women. So eventually women organized their own mission societies and did a remarkable work for the Lord. Soon there was pressure on them to amalgamate with the men's missions. One of the biggest women's societies did this—on the condition that women would have a fair share in decision making. Predictably, it was not long before the men were again running everything and the women had no say. And so it remains in many missions today.

Mention should also be made of the centuries of selfless work done by women in Roman Catholic orders, as missionaries and in the home countries. Many have spread the Christian message, taught children, reared orphans, nursed the sick, and given themselves to prayer all over the world. The best known today is probably Mother Teresa, mentioned earlier, who works with the sisters of her order "among the poorest of the poor" in the despairing slums of Calcutta and of Bangladesh, ministering comfort to the many who are dying and beyond further help. Sisters in Christ, are we willing to give ourselves unselfishly to those in need around us, as Christ's willing servants?

Woman's Place Is Everywhere!
It is encouraging to know that in every field of endeavor

A History of Struggle

today we have successful women. Once we believed that women could do only a few things. Now we know there is hardly anything a woman cannot do if she has the talents and health, and really wants to do it. "A woman's place is in the home," they used to say. And of course that is still a very special and important place for her to be and to work. But she isn't confined to four walls these days. "A woman's place," we now say, "is *everywhere!*" That is a wonderful and liberating thought. The Chinese have a nice proverb, too, which recognizes woman's importance. They say, "Women prop up half the sky."

Often the women have had to struggle against heavy odds to get into professions they wanted to follow. Maria Montessori, the great Italian child-educator and a devout Catholic, was also a doctor. Years ago, when she trained in medicine, she was fortunate to be admitted to the medical school in Rome at all. In fact, she became the first woman doctor in Italy and one of the first in the world. What difficulties she faced! In those days it was not thought "proper" for a woman to study anatomy with young men. So Maria had to come back to school late at night, after all the men had gone home, and do her own studies and dissections of the bodies which doctors have to study!

Despite such setbacks, many women have won a place where they can stand up and be counted, helpers of a needy and dying world. We have women doctors, nurses, teachers, specialists, pediatricians, social workers, secretaries, and homemakers. These are most traditionally "feminine" jobs, though good ones. But we also now see women who are politicians, senators, cabinet ministers, prime ministers, crane drivers, truck drivers, electricians, engineers, mechanics, welders, dentists, lawyers, judges, and scientists. Some are pilots (and remember, there was a time when men were horrified at the thought of a woman even driving a car! In Saudi Arabia today, women are still forbidden by law to drive!).

Truly today, a woman's place is everywhere! Many enlightened Christian women today ensure that their children read books and stories which tell of women and men doing a variety of things outside the tight sex roles and stereotypes. There are a number of books and stories "for free children" now in print, to help break down early barriers of sex and race. Such books show men as well as women doing housework and caring lovingly for small children. They show women as well as men pursuing a variety of careers. They show black people as well as white people, women as well as men, playing leading roles in the community.

Many parents also try to break the stranglehold of stereotypes by giving their children games and toys to encourage a free exploration of the world and of the many exciting possibilities life offers. Little boys as well as girls are encouraged to enjoy and care for dolls if they wish; this may help them become more tender and loving fathers later on. Little girls are allowed to play with toy cars if they wish. Those who observe many small children often say that it is not true that all girls naturally want dolls and all boys cars, etc. It varies with the individual child. Surely Christians should be at the forefront of helping their children grow in freedom towards abundant life, rather than among those who early try to program toddlers for stereotyped future roles. We can stress to our daughters the wonderful rewards and the great importance of homemaking, while still opening up to them the many interesting things women can do, as hobbies or as careers. This way we keep a balance and do not push them to extremes.

Because woman's place is everywhere (or anywhere, as God leads), our opportunities for meaningful service and witness become so much greater. Let us take advantage of these possibilities. A needy world requires that all of us discover our gifts, stir them up and use them to minister where the need is. It may be in unexpected places. A Korean housewife, for example, has a special ministry to bus conductresses in the big city of Seoul. She invites these girls to her home for Bible studies. Other women work with international students studying in Australia, the United States, or Canada. Others serve as preachers and prophetesses, as evangelists, pastors and teachers, as elders and administrators in the church, as workers with youth or the elderly, as choir leaders and organists, as counselors, and as ones who pray and give.

2
The Little Foxes That Steal the Grapes

The year 1975 was International Women's Year. There were many criticisms of extreme elements in the women's movements and of internal fighting and bickering among some women. This is a great pity and shows the need for Christian influence in such movements.

There are always some who spoil what is of itself good and true. In the wonderful movement towards reconciliation, towards a full restoration of woman's God-given dignity and ministry, there are some foxes which "spoil the grapes."

There is a branch of Women's Lib which has overreacted. Because of this, many Christian women have become afraid of any discussion about helping women to greater freedom. They react by running into their shells and refusing even to think about what the women's movement as a whole is saying. As a result, they miss out. They tie themselves up in the old bondage of stereotypes of femininity.

WOMEN IN MINISTRY TODAY

Of course there are extremes in Women's Lib! After all, there are many unbelievers in the movement. Some have misunderstood liberty to mean sexual promiscuity, though the more thinking women (even though non-Christians) realize that this makes a woman *less* free, not more free. A group of lesbians have joined the movement and are wielding considerable influence. Naturally such behavior is repugnant to Christian women. Again, some extremists want to replace the domineering stance of men with domineering women, but that is only to reverse the problem, not to solve it. We read of some "Women's Libbers" who apparently dislike men, lead very un-Christian lives, "burn their bras," wear their hair as if a storm had just hit them, and dress in outlandish ways. They swear a lot (as if that meant liberation!) and perhaps, we suspect, neglect their children for their jobs.

Christian women are naturally turned very far off by such things. So they turn their backs on the whole women's movement, and never realize what they are missing out on. What we need is a Christian women's lib movement—a movement which first of all sees true liberation as offered in Christ, which avoids extremes, while still working for women's greater freedom in the society and the Church. Such a movement will have no time for immorality, and will stress love and faith as the most liberating of qualities. These women will be excellent wives and mothers, as well as fine Christian workers. Some of them will also have jobs and will be competent and happy in them. And, in fact, there are many Christian women who feel this way and are working for our cause.

But let us not assume we have nothing to learn from the women's movement. There are many things wrong with it, but there is also some very good thinking being done. And there is much practical service being given to women in need. These groups provide help of a practical nature to many women, help with child care for many who need to work, counseling in crises, help if they have been attacked or raped, shelter from husbands who beat them, and much more. These are very real needs in our cities. The movement encourages women to be themselves and to develop their gifts to the fullest extent. There are many fine, sensible women in the movement. They are certainly not all extremists! And there are many Christian women working with them as well. There are a variety of different groups working for women; some are hopelessly extreme; many others are sensible, middle-of-the-road organizations doing a lot of good work.

We need, too, to try to understand sympathetically why some women who do not know Christ go to extremes. Some of them have suffered terribly at the hands of cruel, drunken husbands. Some have been deserted by men who cared little for them and nothing for their children. Many have been used and exploited by men. Many Christian women do not really know what such a life is like. Others are angry because their life and careers have been constantly blocked, not by physical violence but by mental cruelty and in other subtle ways. They have not been able to grow and develop as full persons because of prejudice against them. They are often intelligent women who have read the history of women. They are rightly indignant at the shocking record of prejudice and exploitation all through history against their sex. They are upset at what women have suffered in all major religions of the world, including Christianity (for Christians have not always lived up to the teachings of Christ!).

Christian women who dismiss with a shrug the sad and sorry history of women in the world and in our Western societies are simply ignorant. They just do not know the true story of centuries of oppression. This is exactly what the curse on women is all about! The suffering of women goes right back to the Fall. Women who have never felt for their sister in their hearts and never shed a tear as they read the true story of the past, just now becoming available, cannot speak on the matter. They cannot condemn the Women's Libbers, because they just do not know the injustices these women react to. We do not have the right to condemn these women who are struggling for justice if we have never entered their struggle, never felt heart pangs for the history of our sex.

But having said this, we know that the way of the Cross and the way of love is the way upward for women. We have outlined in this book some of these ways forward. We must beware of simplistic, moralistic answers, however, which do not take full account of the real problem. It is easy for Christians to quote a few proof texts on any problems and then dismiss it as solved. Here we can sift the good from the evil, and learn from some of our more radical sisters, just as they must learn the Christian way from us. From our sisters we can, if we are sensitive, learn to feel with others, learn to enter into the agonizing struggle of many women to be free, to be themselves. We can learn that passionate sense of justice, that deep desire for freedom, that enormous strength of mind and determination of purpose which carries them forward, at whatever cost. And we can turn such feelings, such qualities, to a truly Christian service of others.

A lot of Christian groups try to sidestep this problem with too-easy answers. They simply say that we are free spiritually in Christ, for example, and that nothing else matters. But many believers feel that other things *do* matter, and that the freedom we have in the spiritual sphere should break out into practical life in church and society. They do not believe it is enough to be free of sin and then to ignore injustice in society and prejudice in the Church. Christ's reign is to spread through all of life. The prophets of the Old Testament still speak to us today in their impassioned cry for justice, fair dealing, and integrity in practical daily life. They were the champions of the underdogs, as we must be today. We cannot live in a spiritual vacuum. We need very much the message of the prophets today, not only for women's liberty, but for the liberation of many who are oppressed, spiritually and physically. This is not a call to political revolution, as some think. It is a call to spread the influence of the Kingdom and the fullness of redemption into all of life.

God sometimes speaks to us in unexpected ways. In His wisdom and sovereignty He arranges circumstances so that we learn what He wants us to learn. Could not God be speaking to us in some aspects of the women's movements today? (See, for example, a book like Betty Friedan's *The Feminine Mystique,* which contains some useful thinking without the radical politics and language.) And in the same way, have we not an important message for these women?

PART SIX

Single or Married

1
For Singles Only

You single women may feel that this book is written only for married women! It is not! Most of what we have said, except for those parts relating to marriage and family, apply to singles as well. Single women can have just as rich a ministry as their married sisters. A single friend of ours contributes something for singles in this section, so you will know you are not forgotten!

Many women these days are single. Perhaps they were once married or perhaps they have never married. Sometimes they have lost a dear one and have a sad memory to live with. Our society does not always make life easy for those who do not marry. Once upon a time, it was so unusual to stay single that society just did not cater to you at all. It was like that in Bible times. Parents arranged marriages, and only a sick or very ugly woman would be likely to stay single. There was no way for a single woman or a widow to support herself, and no pension. They had to depend on relatives. This is why the early Church took up collections to help widows. Life is still like that in many non-Western countries. Single women are thought to be very odd!

There is still a vestige of that idea around in modern Western countries, but happily, it is fast disappearing. People are beginning to realize that there are various life styles to choose from. It is not inevitable that everyone marry and have children. We may choose to stay single, or we may marry and not have children. We can regulate and space our children to a fair extent if we wish to. All this means greater freedom of choice for women.

These days, too, most single women can support themselves, and if they cannot, the State will grant them a pension of some kind. With so many divorces, many women raise families alone, and the task is difficult and often heart breaking. Christian women are not immune from unhappy marriages and divorces, either. There are widows, with or without families to raise, and there are single women who have never married (and some of them have children). Some of the single remain that way by choice, and some have simply not been asked to marry. This is the reality of our modern world.

Some single women live alone, or just with their children. Some live with friends or family members. But loneliness can still be a real problem. We singles really need to know God, live close to Him, and seek His will for our lives. We need to think through the meaning of being single realistically. Maybe one day we will marry, but as we grow a little older, we realize the chances are not so great. Happiness and fulfillment will depend on recognizing singleness as a real and meaningful way of life. The girl who lives only for the *future* husband, the *future* home she hopes to have, is not facing reality. God may indeed give her a husband, home, and children. But He wants her to be happy in Him, to live in the *now*. Sooner or later we must learn that life is always *now*. It is useless to dwell too much on the past, though it is good to remember happy times and to learn from our mistakes. It is just as useless to live always for the future—"I'll serve God when I get married. I'll be happy when I'm married. When my husband turns up, I'll do this and this . . ." I wonder if they realize, those girls, how many married women say, "When my children are in school I'll serve the Lord," and then, "When the kids are in high school I'll have time for that," and later, "When I have the children off my hands I'll serve God." Before long it is likely to become, "When Jim retires . . ." or really, "Just as soon as I'm dead, I'll be able to . . . !" Living is *now!*

Some Guiding Principles for a Fulfilling Single Life
1. Recognize that being single is a perfectly normal and acceptable way of life. Don't fret about it. It is fine to meet men and to dress attractively and so on. But if you spend all your time trying to attract a man you will probably turn men off! Be yourself. Build your own life. And trust God about that husband!

You must know that God loves and accepts you. You are not inferior because you are single. God hasn't brought you a husband yet because He knows life will be *better* for you single at present, even if it doesn't seem so now.

Don't ever believe that God is shortchanging you. He is the God of abundant life, so trust Him!

2. Stay close to Jesus. Know you are filled with His Spirit. Drink deeply at His wells. He will help you develop as a warm, friendly, spiritual person whose life will bless others. Never allow yourself to grow hard or cynical. We know that men and women are made for each other and complement each other. But wholeness of life is first of all a matter of our relationship to *God,* and only secondarily of our relationship to a *man.* No human can fill God's own place in our hearts. You can be whole in Him, though single.

3. Recognize all the positive things about being single. Don't dwell on the disadvantages. It is natural to miss the love of a husband and children, but don't ever imagine that marriage makes everyone happy. Statistics show that, on the average, single women are actually happier than married women! Paul tells us in 1 Corinthians 7:32-35 that marriage brings many troubles, cares, and distractions from God's work. He tells us that the single person has more time to serve Him. Without a family to care for, you can give more time and love to others who need it—to your own parents, brothers and sisters, nieces and nephews, for a start. It is lovely to be a special aunt! Then you can be a friend to people in need, to the elderly, to invalids, to needy children, and to any others you may wish. You can enjoy more friendships with a bigger variety of people if you work at it. Build warm relationships with people of all ages, from grandmothers to children. Spread joy and thoughtfulness wherever you go, and never

For Singles Only

sit around feeling sorry for yourself.

You will be amazed how your ministry expands! If you love children, help in the Sunday school, baby-sit for friends, or start a Good News Club after school for neighborhood youngsters.

Whatever your gifts are, you can develop them. It is lovely to see husband-wife ministry teams at work, but a single person can have a great ministry, too! Or you can work in a bigger team with others if that suits you.

It will be easier for you than for a married woman to consider the call to full-time service if it comes, and easier to train for it.

If you earn well, you will be able to give generously to God's work. You will have time for much prayer and Bible study if you organize your day well.

And think of the freedom you have as a single woman in today's world. You are probably free to take a job anywhere you choose to live, and to buy or rent a house as you choose. You can travel. You could do short-term service on some mission field, or just visit the missions for interest. You can attend Christian conferences. You can start out on new hobbies, interests, and ventures in a way married people often can't. Be an adventurous single; don't confine yourself to a tiny world out of fear, shyness, or apathy. Give yourself a shake and help build yourself the kind of life you want and develop the kind of ministry God is calling you to!

Another advantage is that you will learn of necessity much about business, current affairs, people, banking, finances, and so on. Lots of married women do not know enough about these things. You will grow as a person and learn to depend on God rather than on a husband. You will have the satisfaction of doing things for yourself, making your own choices with His guidance, planning, and making important decisions. These things help you to become a fuller, more mature person. You will learn to develop in Christ strong inner resources and a full personality, if you approach single life positively. You might be surprised if you knew how many married women secretly envy our freedom! Let's make the most of it!

And remember, the single person in ministry has wonderful precedents! After all, Jesus and Paul were single! So were many other servants of God. Remember that many of the great Christian women we have mentioned were single, too. Catholic clergy and other religious people take vows to remain single because they are sure they can accomplish much more for God that way. Paul says that is true. If you give up being a mother to two or three children, you can be a mother to many children. If you have no family, all those around you can be your family. The Bible says that "God sets the solitary in families" (Ps. 68:6)—you can have many families to enjoy if you walk positively with Him. Banish self-pity. It will ruin your life. Determine to make the most of your present situation, and learn to thank God because He is doing *the best* for you!

A nice side benefit of building a positive single life is that if one day "Mr. Right" does come along, he will find you a far more interesting and stimulating partner than many a young girl who has had little experience of life and has not developed her personality. But don't just build your life "for him"; build it for Christ, for yourself, and for those you can bless with your life. There are always many people far less fortunate, however sad your past may be. Make yourself happy by making them happy.

4. Try to have a rewarding career. For the single girl, it is more important than ever to have a job that you really like. This may be a full-time Christian job. It may be any other worthwhile job. It can be a ministry to the Lord either way, for all of us are really "full-time ministers" to Him, whatever we do. Your work is such an important and central part of your life that you want it to be really worthwhile, and you want to be happy in it. Every job has difficult times, but you should be basically happy in what you are doing. It is more important to find work rewarding than to earn a lot of money. If you are unhappy, ask the Lord about it. Perhaps there could be some change in your work for the same company, or maybe you should look for another job.

In fact, it is better to think of a career or a vocation than just a job. Look ahead. Don't simply mark time in the hope that when the handsome husband arrives you can quit work. You may not marry and—remember—life is *now*, not "when I am married." A satisfying career develops and uses skills and talents. It builds your personality. You feel you are doing something worthwhile for the community. You grow with your career and find advancement over the years. For a rewarding career, you need to start in the right place so you can work up (not always easy for a woman, so pick your place of employment carefully).

Very often, you also need specific training. If you lack the skills for the job you want, it will be easier for you than for married people to acquire them. In times of unemployment, you may hesitate to leave a good job for full-time training. However, if you save enough, you can take the risk of moving out and looking for more training or another job, should you feel strongly that you want to do this.

There are many facilities, however, for furthering your education part-time while you are still working. Life is now all right, but that does not mean we forget about the future. We should plan ahead for long-term satisfaction. We cannot control whether or not we will meet that handsome six-footer and get married. But to a fair degree, we can control our future by prayerfully planning. One way we can help realize our goals is to get training for "that job you always wanted." There are numerous night schools, technical colleges, and correspondence schools. Many cost little or nothing. They offer a whole range of exciting possibilities—trades, professional training, general education, high-school education (if you missed out on that), university degrees on a part-time basis, or just general interest and hobby subjects. And you meet people in such courses. You can also study Bible subjects part time by correspondence, night school, or theological education by extension.

Plan for the career you want and to be the kind of person God wants you to be. Work towards something worthwhile and find the satisfaction of achieving your goals step by step.

5. Learn to make friends. C.S. Lewis, in *The Four Loves*, says there are few people so pathetic as those who just "want friends" and never seem to make them. He says that these people forget that "friendship has to be *about* something." That is very wise.

Usually our closest friends are those we get to know as we work on some project together, study together, share an interest together, or serve the Lord in team ministry. Don't go around just vaguely "looking for friends" if you are lonely. Get involved in activities and in ministry, and friends will "just happen." Go to places where people are. Join organizations which serve others, share the gospel, or simply share an interest. Go to some adult classes to learn whatever interests you—Bible subjects, photography, gardening, languages, typing, home decoration, cooking, history, ecology, ham radio, drama, creative writing, or painting. The list is endless. Try something new, and you will meet new people and make new friends in the process.

The Bible has lots of good advice about making friends (and this applies as much to married as to single women). Using your concordance, look up the various references to "friend" or "friends" in Proverbs for a start. One good piece of advice is in Proverbs 18:24, "A man [or woman!] that hath friends must show himself friendly." To make friends and keep them, we must be warm, outgoing and friendly. We must work at friendship. We must not cling to people or become too dependent on them. "Clingy," insecure friends are usually only tolerated, not welcomed. Building a genuine friendship takes time and effort. The effort is worth it. Rich friendships are among the choicest relationships in life. We minister to each other in friendship.

So, single sister, don't spend your time wishing, dreaming, or chasing rainbows. Don't chase after happiness, because you will find it is an elusive butterfly. The more you chase happiness, the more she seems to elude you. Happiness is really the byproduct of something else, of serving God and being in His will, of having deep and abiding interests, of close friendships, and of personal achievement and a sense of doing something worthwhile with your life. It is not just an accumulation of pleasures and outings, of parties and dates, as many seem to believe.

And when you make your friends, be loyal to them. Don't be disloyal to some of your friends by giving them less attention than those friends you think could be "eligible"! It can be a temptation to put aside, for example, a planned outing with an old lady when a handsome young man wants to take you out! But in most cases, that is not really being fair to your elderly friend. Be fair and loyal and life will be better in the long run!

6. Develop deep interests and a real purpose in life. The Lord can help you do this. He wants your life to serve His Kingdom in your own special way. Like all of us, you need to determine where your gifts lie, develop them, and seek God's leading for your particular sphere of ministry. You may do several different things, but ideally, there will be some focus—some general direction in which you are moving—in line with your gifts. You won't try to do everything or to take on too much. You will concentrate

mainly (not legalistically) on those ministries which accord with your gifts. Don't try to be a square peg in a round hole just because someone wants you to do something. Try not to spread yourself too thin, and be honest with yourself about where your gifts do and do not lie!

One of the most interesting things that some social scientists have discovered in recent years has been that a very fundamental need of the human being is his or her need for at least one deep interest in life. A Christian will have her most basic interest in doing her part for the Kingdom of God. But we may properly have other deep interests, too. These need not always be specifically Christian interests, for, to a believer, the whole world and all the interesting and exciting things in it belong to God, anyway. We do not therefore have to confine our interests to "religious" matters. A healthy person has a variety of interests, and these can all glorify God; and they can also present opportunities to meet others and to be a witness to Christ.

Studies have found that many housewives suffer during middle age with "the problem that has no name" (see Betty Friedan's book mentioned earlier for a fuller explanation of this). They seem unhappy and discontented for no special reason. Sometimes these discontented women begin to smoke cigarettes, drink too much coffee, or watch too much TV, and some even begin to drink excessively and misuse drugs. They seem to lack purpose and moorings. There is a vague feeling of dissatisfaction, and yet they are well and are reasonably happy in their family lives. We know, of course, that this vague emptiness and lack of purpose is often a characteristic of those who do not have Christ in their lives. The symptoms are not confined to unbelievers, however, for Christian women—and men—often suffer from the same problem.

Basically, these people's lives lack any serious *interests*. Real interests give direction to our lives and help to define our personality. A serious interest is one that we take far enough to develop real skills and to initiate projects. Many men find this kind of practical interest and purpose in their jobs, though of course many others do not. Housewives, however, often lack such deep and abiding interests. Naturally, they are interested in their families, but their children begin to grow up and leave home, and they know that they cannot live forever for the children only. Housework itself is often not as challenging and rewarding as it once was, because we have so many modern conveniences. This is one reason some women are returning to growing their own food, spinning their own wool, weaving cloth, making their own bread, butter and even soap, and so on. These are all interesting things to do, but they hardly solve "the problem that has no name."

Not all women have this difficulty, of course, but it is very common. Christian women may have these troubles, too. Even though Christ is central in their lives, they have not been able to work out any really challenging plan of service for Him. And they may lack other deep interests. Many women simply dabble in interests. They do a little sewing, and attend a pottery class for a few weeks, followed by some dabbling in golf. And they may not be given opportunity to do much more than dabble in Christian service, either. Their Christian service, therefore, may be rather haphazard and "bitsy"—bringing flowers once a month, attending a ladies' group, helping out in this or that. Their service in the community may be much the same. All these are good things to do. But they are not sufficient to constitute a challenge. There is no big plan, no project, no big cause we are working for. There is no real direction. There is little in such work which gives us a deep sense of satisfaction or worth. Subconsciously perhaps we know we are just "dabbling" in living. And we want more, but we don't know how to get it.

Here I am talking to all women. The concept of the serious interest (or interests) is crucial. It can help us if we grasp hold of it. The happiest and most fulfilled people are those who feel they have a calling and a mission in life. They have purpose and drive. They take risks more than they opt for safety and comfort. What a challenge to the vital use of our ministries for the Lord! Think about it!

Also, think, too, about other important, though secondary interests in life. What natural interests and talents have you, which you could develop and do something with? Everybody needs to feel that she has built up some knowledge and skills that are valuable, and that she can use these to help others. A serious interest is more than something we "dabble" in. It is a career or a hobby we take seriously. It involves learning something, either informally from others, by teaching ourselves, or by receiving training. Some people have enough perseverance to teach themselves really valuable skills. Most do not, and the only way they will acquire them is to take a course of study and then to use what they learn. Learning itself can be enormously satisfying. Don't let any unhappy school experiences put you off. If you have never felt the joy of learning something new, the power of being able to do and think things previously impossible, you have missed something!

Those who criticize Christian women for pursuing careers when they have families to care for may not realize how important outside work may be to a woman. If she has skills to build a real career, she may find this enormously satisfying and may be a much better wife and mother as a result. Much of the time, serious skills are the kind that are saleable. Those who develop skills and interests but do not carry these to the point where anyone would want to employ them in this field have rarely developed them very seriously. No matter, if all you want is an exciting hobby. But only serious interests and skills are usually able to provide the kind of satisfaction that helps us fulfill our full potential and avoid the "problem which has no name." That mother who "doesn't need to work" but chooses to do so may well be insuring herself and her family against the middle-age blues. She is a sharp, thinking person who happens to need outside stimulus very much. It may be hard for women who do not need this stimulus to understand, but for multitudes of women, that is how it is. The need is for them an absolutely basic one. They are not being selfish. They know that if they are unable to fulfill this need for purpose, deep interests, and real direction, they will become bored and frustrated. They will be a trial to their husbands and

For Singles Only

make home unpleasant for their children.

Sometimes young mothers, in the throes of the excitement of marriage and new babies, fail to understand how other, older women feel such a strong need for outside interests. Later, probably, they will understand.

Remember, people are different. This is not everyone's problem. Many women find all the direction and fulfillment they need in the challenges of home life. Many others do not. They must try to understand each other, and not to condemn. But it does seem fairly sure that *all* people, whether they recognize it or not, do have this basic need for abiding interests and purpose. They find it in different ways. The single woman needs to be very much aware of this need. She cannot meet it with a husband and family. But she can meet it in many other exciting ways!

7. Make yourself a home to live. It need not be expensive and it need not be your own, though many singles like to purchase their own small home or unit over the years. But it does need to be *you* and to express your interests and personality (and that of anyone sharing with you). It should be comfortable and "homey," somewhere you can relax and be yourself.

You can find much pleasure in decorating your home simply, to be what you want. A home to come back to after a day at work is very reassuring. It helps give you a base to work from. And it is nice to be able to invite people in.

Set reasonable but not unrealistic standards for keeping your home clean and tidy. If you always leave things in a mess, you will find it gets you down, and you will be ashamed if friends drop in. A little work regularly and a big clean now and again are all that is needed. A nice, friendly, clean home does lots for good mental health. Be sure to cook for yourself properly too. Those who live alone, in particular, are often likely to neglect proper meals. Don't go on crazy diets, but be sensible about losing weight, if you need to. See that you get plenty of fresh fruits and vegetables, protein foods, dairy products, and perhaps a vitamin supplement. Also look after your health in other ways, with adequate sleep and exercise. Unless you stay healthy, your ministry will not amount to much!

If you board with a family, or live at home, try to make your own room specially yours, a room that reflects your personality and which you enjoy being in.

All these little things play an important part in your health and happiness, and so enhance your ministry as a Christian single!

2

The Beautiful Ministry of the Homemaker

The ministry of the homemaker can be for some a beautiful and satisfying calling. The instruction Paul gave to husbands and wives in Ephesians 5 was never meant to be a matter of law but of love, a team ministry in love. Husband and wife have a ministry to each other, a beautiful ministry. Paul is speaking here of Christian couples who are equally yoked together, not of unsaved and unequally yoked husbands and wives. There is instruction given for these situations also, but it is different from that given to equally yoked husbands and wives. It is a real ministry of the Lord when a husband shows the same love to his wife as Christ did to the Church. And what a beautiful thing it is when a wife shows the same submission (honor and respect) to her husband as she does to the Lord. This is also a real ministry of the Lord.

Then the love flowing forth from the father and mother towards the children ministers to them in the

Lord. How precious children are to the heart of the Father-God; how His heart aches to love them through us with His love! I call our family the first fruits of our ministry, the others to whom we minister, the harvest. The first fruits always belonged to the Lord; they received the first consideration and came above all other fruits. The harvest ministry is second. I cherish my first fruits, and I love the harvest as well.

A husband and wife have something to share on every level with each other and can be a perfect team together. Children also have something to share in the family unit. We cannot reduce God's plan for husbands and wives to a set of authoritarian rules. He has pointed out the way of love to us, to follow as we choose. And there never will be only one particular way for all husbands and wives to live. Let each family dwell together according to their knowledge of one another; this will certainly differ from one family to another. What is a happy life style for one couple may be misery for another. No one has a right to force his opinions and personal preferences upon another's marriage. Christ died to set us free from this bondage, to find our way in Him.

Now let us look at the teachings of Paul concerning husbands and wives. We shall first look into Ephesians 5:21-33. We must note the background of the apostles—the husband could destroy his wife or daughters if he chose, by the Roman law (but not by God's law). Thus, it behooved Paul to instruct the Body of Christ in the truth for their own protection. He is giving instruction to the Church concerning husbands and wives. The first thing we note is that Paul speaks equally to husbands and wives. This is clearly understood from the manner in which Paul addresses both husbands and wives, and is more clarified as we study the following verses.

Verse 22 says, "Wives, submit yourselves unto your own husbands, as unto the Lord" (the *agape* love principle). The Greek word for "submit" has various meanings, but in this particular verse we have *hupotasso,* meaning "to place oneself under, to subject oneself," with the idea of honoring and reverencing another. This does not mean becoming subservient. It is a loving deference to the other's wishes, humbly putting another's concerns first. Notice that verse 21 tells men and women to submit *to each other* in a general sense; so whatever submission is asked of wives is of *the same kind* (because the same word is used) as that which all believers should give to one another (and that also includes men to women). It does not imply, as some say, that the husband must take all the initiatives, make all the important decisions, or always get his own way! The wife is a person, too. Look at the active, vigorous housewife/businesswoman in Proverbs 31! We must also read Ephesians 5 remembering that Roman law made the husband head and held *him* responsible for his wife and family, should they break the law. This made the wife responsible to her husband as well as to the Lord in a manner which does not apply to the same degree today.

This differs from Genesis 3:16: "And thy desire shall be to thy husband, and he shall rule over thee." That was part of the curse!

WOMEN IN MINISTRY TODAY

Now to continue with Ephesians 5:22: "as unto the Lord." To do this as a ministry unto the Lord is a very deep and beautiful principle. When a man and woman completely give themselves to the Lord, to the point where they can say, "I am completely yours, Lord; you are first; you are before my husband or wife, my children, my ministry," when they are dead to self (Col. 3:1-3), then the Lord is able to do great things with their lives. God, through us, will love and honor the other partner. He will work through us individually to meet the needs of our partner. He knows the cooperation needed in marriage better than we ever could. He also helps us meet the needs of our children as we yield to Him.

When Christ begins to live His life through us, there is no neglect, no lack of love or understanding. We are dead to self and alive to God (Gal. 2:20-21), thus allowing Christ to live His life through us. This is the principle of "as unto the Lord." We are to do this service and minister this love in our homes as a ministry not only to others but to the Lord himself.

But notice, we need more than our own efforts to do this. Christ's strength, which knows no limits, is the strength we need. Let us look more at the practical side of our daily lives as homemakers.

I found this letter recently in a women's magazine:

> From the time I married I battled against the housewife image, and worked until the birth of my third child. This gave me contact with the mainstream. After "retiring," I felt left out, and bored, so I rushed

to find social and intellectual outlets. Recent economic hardships have forced me to give up my social activities and adult classes and to become "just a housewife." Yet the pleasure and contentment I have found is really unbelievable. I sew, knit, preserve, and get tremendous satisfaction from an ambitious job's completion. My family benefits from having a more relaxed Mom and I realize that there will be time for me to catch up on previous interests after the children have grown.

"Contented Mom"

Being a wife and mother has many rewards, and being a good homemaker is a fulfilling ministry to the Lord. Never let anyone say that work in the home is not important. This woman found joy and reward in the everyday duties of her home.

We must notice, however, to be realistic, that some women are more suited to this ministry by nature than are others. Some have real spiritual gifts as well as natural talents in this direction. Such a woman, we sometimes say, has the gift of being a "mother in Israel." Perhaps she ministers to a spiritual family as well as to her natural family.

Women are different from one another. And we are different at various times in our lives, too. At one time, the writer of the above letter found her greatest satisfaction in combining homemaking with an outside job. Later, she quit her job and found fulfillment in homemaking plus certain activities. And finally, she found it very nice just to be able to stay at home and live a more relaxed life. Later, she hints, she may go back to an outside job as well.

It is not that one of these ways of life is better than all the others. It depends on the woman, and it may also change with the years. God gives us freedom to choose our life style, so long as we make certain that our families are properly cared for. Most married women have a choice whether they work outside the home full time, part time or not at all. That is more choice than our husbands usually have! We should be thankful for the freedom of choice we enjoy. It may be good for us to experience several styles of living during our lives.

There is no need to be frustrated or brought into bondage by the things that others say. For example, some say that women are born to be homemakers, and imply that therefore, *every* woman should be first-class at housework and child care. The fact is, and simple observation can verify it, that some women are much better suited to this work than others. Some women love it and others heartily dislike it. All men are not good at the same tasks. Why should all women be excellent housekeepers? All of us can do our best, of course, and we can keep the home clean, tidy, and a pleasant place to be in. But some will always be better than others. Some of us just can't sew a straight seam. We can cook good plain meals, but our cakes sometimes sag in the middle, our dinners sometimes burn, and we never expect to win prizes for our jams, jellies, or preserves!

Some of us take longer to clean than others. Our children seem to get dirty quicker than other people's and

The Beautiful Ministry of the Homemaker

our laundry doesn't shine and gleam like those terribly white washes in the soap powder ads. Our children don't seem as clever or as well behaved as someone else's, and we often feel guilty or depressed because our floors don't reflect our faces and we can't meet our husbands looking fresh as a daisy in the evening.

It is important to be realistic with ourselves so we do not suffer from unnecessary condemnation. We should assess our talents and do the best we can without fretting over the fact that we do not sew, cook, or decorate our homes as beautifully as some other women. Often we imagine that our friends and neighbors run their homes in a far smoother manner than is in fact the case. We build up unreal expectations from too many television ads showing forever-young housewives with fabulous figures sailing through their housework in their best clothes and remaining happy and sparkling at all times. Their houses look too perfect to be lived in! Houses are for living in first of all, not for showy display. Even some books which are popular with Christians are unrealistic.

For example, lots of Christian women in recent times have been reading *The Total Woman*. Many say it is a revelation and has helped them greatly. Good. There are many good suggestions in the book. A lot of it is common sense. In particular, it encourages women who may have been unnecessarily prudish or fearful to be more adventurous in their love lives with their husbands. That is excellent advice. Many Christian women have had unnecessary fears and hang-ups in this area of their lives, and they need to know that God does not intend it that way, and that their husbands will usually respond well to a more creative and less inhibited approach in this area.

One problem with the book is that it seems to assume that the woman's *only* real role in life is that of homemaker, and that all "normal" or "good" women stay home all day. In fact, many women work part or full time and are the better for it. Even their homes are often better for it. Being a full-time housewife is one very good life style. Working as well is another good life style. And the wife who works may be tired at night. She may not always be able to meet her husband at the door in party clothes, having just had a long soak in a bubble bath! If a woman stays home all day, she may still not be able to do that!

At times the suggestions are rather absurd. The author mentions the embarrassment caused, for example, when a very scantily-clad graduate of one of her courses greeted a repairman at the door! She had assumed it was her husband at the door! Surely this very real danger makes it impractical for wives to greet their husbands this way too often! They will need to be absolutely sure it is he who is ringing the bell! Again, for mother to parade about the house dressed like a siren may be fine when the children are babies, or when a woman has no children. But how many of us would feel like going about the house almost naked in front of older children when dad's return from the office draws near! Such ideas, in a practical situation, seem rather silly. The same is true of phoning your husband at the office to whisper words of love in his ear—as the author herself admits, it is easy to get

The Beautiful Ministry of the Homemaker

connected with another man in the office by mistake!

Christian women ought not to join "crazes," but should rather sift out what is useful and God-honoring, and scrap the rest! We need not feel frustrated and condemned just because we do not cut the figure of the "total woman" or of the glamorous and oh-so-efficient housewives on the TV ads. Let's do our best and be ourselves!

Some modern women will try to tell you that you must be unfulfilled if you stay at home. But that depends on the person. It could be that you would benefit from a part or full-time outside job. But if you are happy staying at home, that is fine. Homemaking can be a full-time career and a very rewarding one. It is certainly more challenging than many jobs for which one is paid. Most who stay at home, however, will want to have some outlets—some opportunities to work for the Lord in the church or community, some hobbies and chances to socialize. That is good, so long as you do not take on too much. Many full-time homemakers enjoy taking some adult courses or improving their own education by reading or Bible study.

On the other hand, Christians even more often condemn the mother who works outside the home. But you need not be afraid of those who claim terrible harm will befall your children because of your job. Very often, working mothers feel very guilty. Other people suggest they are only working for selfish reasons—to buy more material things. Any time something goes wrong in the home or a child gets into some trouble, the mother tends to blame her job, forgetting that full-time mothers have exactly the same problems.

Contrary to what is often said, psychological studies do *not* prove that your children will be harmed if you work. The factors which lead to good homes and well-adjusted children are far more complex than whether or not mother has a job. What *is* undeniably essential is that children not be left on their own, unsupervised. There must be *someone* to care for them kindly and firmly while you are at work or for after school. But that someone does not have to be mother. It may be grandmother, auntie, a neighbor or a paid housekeeper. It may also be dad, if his hours are different than yours!

Some children benefit from spending time with people other than mother. And many mothers are better off working. If they stay home all day, they become bored and frustrated, and they could take out these frustrations on their families. Many child abusers are full-time mothers! Again, it depends on the woman. Some love being at home all day, and others detest it. We ought not to criticize either kind of woman, provided the necessary housework and loving child care is done. People are simply different!

The point is that, provided children are properly and lovingly cared for, it is not just the *amount* of time we spend with our children that counts. It is the *quality* of that time.

A Word About Roles

One thing this book stresses is that people are individuals. People are different. All of God's creation evidences a glorious variety. We have not just one but many kinds of trees, not one but countless kinds of scenery on earth, not one but many breeds of dog, not one but many races of man. God makes people brown, yellow, white, black, and red because He loves that kind of variety. He makes us men *and* women because that makes the world so much more interesting!

He makes personalities so different, too! One of the major things which distinguishes human beings from the animals is that we have much more definite and different personalities than they do. People have different looks, different interests, different talents, different likes and dislikes. This is part of the wonder of creation.

For too long, we have tended to put men and women into role straightjackets. All men should be tough, we sometimes imagine, like the "Marlboro" men in the ads. Men are stereotyped. To be manly is thought to mean never showing your feelings, disliking housework, being good at carpentry and mechanical things, following sporting events with gusto, and loving nothing better than to be underneath a car with a variety of tools. Women are, however, squeezed into role expectations even more tightly than men. All women are supposed to love children, be naturally good homemakers, love sewing and cooking, cry easily, be illogical, and work best in subservient positions.

Too often, men or women who do not live up to these expectations feel they are "unfeminine" or "unmanly." They may be teased or even treated badly. More importantly, they often feel guilty and think they are somehow unnatural. They may twist themselves out of their true shapes by trying to conform to role expectations. Life may be hard for the man who loves small children and has deep feelings, or for the woman who would rather be with adults than toddlers, dislikes housework, and dreams of driving cranes for a living!

Role stereotypes, while they have some uses, often constrict people's lives and force them to be other than themselves. Many marriages are unhappy because two people are trying to live out expected roles instead of being themselves. Some roles can be very damaging. Psychologists have shown, for example, that the "manly" trait of never expressing your feelings is a dangerous one. When feelings are bottled up and not released, when no true communication takes place between a man and other people or between a man and his wife because of this role expectation, the man's mind becomes like a rumbling volcano. It may erupt at any time. Relationships and marriages are damaged. This is thought to be one of the reasons women on the average live longer than men— the male role, says psychologist Sidney Jourard in *The Transparent Self,* is a lethal one. Jesus was a true man as well as God. But He was not ashamed to show His feelings. The Bible records that He wept.

Women's "feminine" role expectations also often severely truncate their lives and prevent them from launching out and trying new things. Many women are so afraid of being thought "masculine" or "aggressive" that they live passively rather than as self-activating people. They try to live vicariously through their husbands and children instead of living as themselves and encouraging their families to do the same in a natural, healthy manner. We can be ourselves and still live together in harmony and love. That is God's way. These role expectations are one reason many women fear they must not take outside jobs. They forget about the ideal woman in Proverbs, who was not only a good housewife and mother but also a competent businesswoman!

These days, some of the sterotypes are breaking down and people are becoming more free. Some men are becoming kindergarten teachers, and they and the children love it! In many families, husbands and wives share both the housework and the earning. Fathers are encouraged to spend more time with their children and to cease looking upon child care as solely the job of the woman. And there are very few jobs in the world which women have not done successfully. If a woman wishes to be a carpenter or a mechanic, an engineer or an executive, why not? We have examples of women doing all these and many more things, and doing them well. Well-adjusted women do not fear losing some rather flimsy thing called "femininity." Who defines what is "feminine," anyway? The definition is different in every culture. In New Guinea it is feminine to be physically strong, to carry most of the heavy loads, and to do most of the heavy gardening and agricultural work. Christ's women do not have to act like men. But they can expand the traditional limitations of what was considered feminine! They are sure enough of their womanhood to launch out and be themselves. Christ can set us free in these ways if we will but let Him!

Many conservative Christians frequently stress the

idea that God created men and women to fulfill quite separate roles. These are "natural" roles. If these roles are blurred, they say, we will soon have a dreary, "unisex" world, where men and women dress and act the same way. Worse, they claim, this will encourage homosexuality, because women will become domineering or debased and men will become effeminate.

Family life, these people say, is terribly threatened by a breakdown in traditional roles. Children will be neglected. Homes will break up. Indeed there is almost no end to the evils which these prophets of doom tell us will ensue if we question traditional roles. All of society will be endangered.

What do we say to this?

First, it is very hard to show from the Bible that God did in fact establish such distinct roles for men and women. Obviously, there are biological differences between men and and women that determine their roles to some extent. There are probably also some psychological differences, though it is difficult to prove that these are inborn rather than culturally determined, since psychological traits differ so much from one individual to another, and since male-female characteristics and roles vary greatly from one country to another. Christians who support greater freedom from rigid sex roles are in no way denying that there are important differences between men and women. They accept this and want each sex to continue to make its full contribution to the world. But they want men to contribute their special gifts and insights to the home as well as to the wider world, and they want women to contribute their special talents and understanding to the wider world as well as to the home. We should not follow the extremists here, but seek to find a responsible approach.

The truth is that role stereotypes encourage a drab and dreary sameness, especially among women. Human beings can develop far richer personalities when they are free to build their own roles, not according to a stereotype but according to their God-given interests, gifts, and talents. When the rigid roles are removed, a woman can take an interest in car engines, politics, football, or theology without in any way feeling "unfeminine." And her husband can freely develop his love of small children, an interest in music or poetry, a hobby of knitting, or a career as a preschool teacher without feeling he has lost any "masculinity."

Back at the beginning, God gave to both man and woman together the combined roles of parenting and of ruling the earth and developing the whole range of agriculture, industry, animal husbandry, and other cultural occupations which characterize a human civilization (Gen. 1:28). He created them equal—one species, human beings, with a subdivision between male and female (Gen. 1:27). Their common humanity was more important than the differences between the sexes. Eve was taken from Adam's side to stand alongside him, not from his head to rule over him or from his foot to stand beneath him.

Proverbs 31, as we have seen, gives no support to the rigid role theory. This ideal woman is deeply involved both in her home and in business and the affairs of the wider world. And her husband and family love her for it. This is no child-wife! None of her duties is neglected.

The Bible stresses the importance of both the mother and the father in the home and in child care (e.g., Deut. 6:6-9). It also specifically tells both parents to rule the home (Gen. 18:19; 1 Tim. 3:4-5; 1 Tim. 5:14—most translations are too weak here; the verb means "rule the home with a strong hand").

In no way are we to commend neglect of home and children or propose a dreary world in which all people are the same! Rather, we are to look for richer, more wholesome homes led by parents who have themselves developed a deep sense of responsibility, a profound faith, a mature outlook, and full and interesting personalities. There is excellent evidence, biblical and practical, that such homes, far from leading to the breakdown of society, are fine places for children to grow up and contribute enormously to the strengthening of all that is good and worthwhile in our society.

Making the Most of Homemaking

Let us avoid extremes in all of our thinking. And let us recognize and rejoice in the differences among people. But most of us women, whether we work outside the home or not, will still have a homemaking task. We may, for instance, choose to stay home while our children are very young, but wish to work full or part time when they reach school age. For many, that is a good compromise and promises a taste of "both worlds."

The Beautiful Ministry of the Homemaker

Whether it is done on a full or a part-time basis, homemaking can be interesting and rewarding, even if you are not naturally very talented in this direction. There are a few women who really cannot cope with housework, or whose outside jobs make it almost impossible for them to do all the housework as well. They may wish to get in some household help. Then the spare time they have can go to family activities rather than to cleaning, washing, and scrubbing. This is a good solution for some.

There are many good books that can help you become a better homemaker and mother. Books of household hints and sensible recipes are a start. And if you are new to housekeeping and child rearing, there is often an experienced relative or friend who can give a lot of good advice. There are plenty of outlets for the creative expression of your personality in the way you decorate the home, too—in the colors you choose and the pictures you and your husband enjoy. One book that will give you lots of ideas for creative homemaking and mothering is Edith Schaeffer's *Hidden Art* (Norfolk Press).

Rearing your children is always a creative challenge. You can spend time teaching them the basic truths of God's Word and important moral precepts. Discipline them firmly but lovingly and build in them respect for their parents and for one another. It is very important that discipline be consistent, and that parents not argue about the children's behavior in front of them.

Help your children to learn to think for themselves and to ask thoughtful questions. Discuss with them current events and TV shows they watch, and allow them to share in some of the family decision making. Remember, the Bible says that you, as well as your husband, are to rule your home.

You can introduce your family to all the wonders of God's grace and also to the beauty of the world around. Be sure to teach them early the joys of nature—visits to the seaside, climbing in the mountains, fishing in a lake or a stream, bushwalking, visits to a farm. They can learn to look after pets, visit a zoo and discover new kinds of animals, try horse riding, or learn about many of nature's wonders, past and present. Walks around rock pools at the beach, looking at the varied sea creatures, are interesting to children, especially if you have a book which tells you more about them. Happy are those children who early in life are introduced to the wonderful variety of natural things, who love to spend time in the open and to develop their knowledge by reading more about nature. Wherever you happen to live, try to make the most of the opportunities in this direction for your children.

Then there is the wonderful world of literature and the arts. If your children do not learn any musical instrument at school, try to arrange lessons for them, or learn a simple instrument and teach them yourself. Encourage them to play many hymns and choruses and some of the beautiful Scriptures in song. They will be able to put these talents to good use as they grow older. And the words will stay with them long after they have forgotten their Sunday school memory verses! But teach them to enjoy many other kinds of music, too. Encourage your children to enjoy good art. When you can, arrange visits to the public galleries and share art books from the library with them, according to their age and ability to understand. Tell them stories about famous musicians and artists. Let there be good art and lots of fine music in the home. Children who grow up with these things from an early age will not forget them. Our enjoyment of music and art should be like our enjoyment of food—we need both our heavy meals and light snacks!

What a wealth of literature is open to us. First and foremost is the Bible. From an early age, our children can learn the stories and teaching of God's Word. There is also plenty of good children's literature. You will find lots of good suggestions for the younger children in Gladys Hunt's delightful book *Honey for a Child's Heart: The Imaginative Use of Books in Family Life.* The book is written from a Christian perspective.

A good mother or father also helps children develop hobbies and creative interests. Where possible, such parents take their children on outings to help them learn about the community they live in. Encourage your children to dress up (keep a "dressing-up box" of old clothes just for fun). They can make up plays and put on concerts, with mother and father as an appreciative audience, of course! Give them the chance to paint, draw, model, do some creative writing, make music. There are sports and other games they can follow. Remember, children with lots of interests and hobbies are far less likely to get into trouble in their teen years. Some

WOMEN IN MINISTRY TODAY

Christian parents seem to think that such things are unimportant—how wrong they are!

Many families these days find that television takes up too much of their children's time. There are some excellent programs on TV, but there is much rubbish as well. You will need to police the use of the TV set in your home; it must be your servant, not your master. Parents who spend all their time in front of the set and never engage in conversation or creative activities will soon find their children follow their example. What you do sets a far more powerful example than what you say! But the TV needs to be regulated in a positive rather than a negative way. It should not be the cause of constant arguments. One good idea is to allow a certain number of hours of viewing each week, sit down with the children when the television guide arrives, and plan with them a suitable week's viewing. You can mark their programs with a see-through felt marker. Make sure you see one or two episodes of each show they watch, so that you have a good idea what your children are looking at.

Seeing too much violence has been proven to be bad for children, though some seek to pretend it does no harm. The massive efforts of the Parent-Teacher Associations in America to prevent so much violence in children's programs is an encouraging sign. With young children, you need to remember that the news bulletins often contain reports of tragedy and violence; it may be better for them not to be watching with you. Encourage your family to view with a purpose and not just to "kill time." Do what you can to work for the improvement of the standards in programs being shown in your area. It is everyone's responsibility.

Many families like to have a special "family evening" regularly. It is a time when you talk together, join in reading aloud, parlor games, and other activities. Cold winter nights by the fireside used to be a favorite time for such activities, which help bring families closer together. In summer, it might be an early evening swim or walk. And any time, it might include having the children help you prepare a special meal. (Don't forget to teach your sons as well as your daughters to cook—everyone should know how to feed himself! The same goes for darning socks and sewing on buttons, and for performing simple household repairs; girls need to learn the latter as well as boys!)

A wise Christian parent takes an active interest in the children's education, too, and if possible works in the local parent-teacher organization. These days, many stay-home mothers spend an hour or two each week assisting in the elementary classroom, listening to children read, supervising free play or helping keep order on an excursion. If your school asks for such help and you can give it, it will help bind home and school more closely together and will give you many interesting insights into what your child is learning. If the new math or some of the other modern teaching methods are a mystery to you, attend lectures for parents at the school or borrow a book from the library to help you understand. It is good to give limited help with homework and to ensure that the child has a quiet place to study. But don't do the work for him.

WOMEN IN MINISTRY TODAY

Many Christian parents would like to send their children to Christian schools, and there are more of these around today. Others cannot afford that, or prefer the public schools. A lot will depend on your situation. If the school is too restrictive, the children may revolt against Christianity in later life. The school should prepare them for the realities of life in a largely non-Christian world. It may introduce the real world slowly, but it must not be a "hothouse." The same is true of Christian colleges in the United States. (These do not exist in most other English-speaking countries.)

It is important these days for your child to stay in school as long as possible. A good education is essential to a good job these days. But there are cases where it is best to let a restless youngster leave school, and then help him to continue his education part time or evenings at a later date when he has learned the importance of a full high-school training.

Every young person should be given training for some job or profession. If you can help him get "two strings in his bow," so much the better. This goes for our daughters as well as our sons. It is very shortsighted to say these days that the education of girls is less important than that of boys because "they will just get married." Being a good homemaker requires plenty of education, too! Education is not only for a job, but to develop one's mind and spirit to fullest potential, to help a person have abundant life.

Good vocational training, however, always stands a girl as much as a boy in good stead. It is an excellent investment and does wonders for the self-image, too. So many wives and mothers these days either need to work or want to work. Sadly, many are divorced or deserted. The woman with proper vocational training can move out and support her family properly if this should happen. Impress on your children the importance of completing some vocational training before they marry if at all possible. It is so much harder when one is married and has a family to support. Many girls thoughtlessly leave their education in midstream to marry, and regret it later.

Some Ideas for Earning

The woman who does not wish to work full time but would like a little extra income needs to think imaginatively about the possibilities. Remember the "many irons" held in the fire by our friend in Proverbs 31!

If you like meeting people, you may enjoy being a part-time sales representative for one of those firms that sells cosmetics or cleaning products from door to door. Perhaps you would prefer the ministry of selling Christian literature from door to door (could you arrange this with a bookstore in your area?). Or you may do as some of my friends have done and arrange with a bookstore or publisher to take small displays of Christian books to local fairs or shows, exhibitions, fetes, Christian camps, and so on.

Think of any special talents you have or could acquire which might provide the makings of your own little business. My mother, for instance, learned to make delicious candies. Her sweets sold well and were popular all over town. My aunts used to make a delightful kind of golliwog doll, and they earned a tidy income selling these to eager customers. Many women do dressmaking, knitting, leatherwork, painting, or crafts. Some do cake decorating or sell their jams and preserves. How about a little business selling sandwich lunches to business people? One young man had his own business while still at school. He made chocolate crackles and old-fashioned ginger beer for sale. Students who miss home cooking are often good customers for goodies like these!

Many women learn to type and take in typing jobs or other office work. It is handy to have something you can do at home. Those who learn to type theses and term papers can do a good business if they live near a college or university and advertise on campus.

Home crafts are always popular. Some women make pottery beads, jewelry, vases, and so on. Some learn more sophisticated crafts, such as batik, silk-screen painting (T-shirts sell very well!), or etching. Such things, and ordinary painting and ceramics work, can be learned at classes.

If you have enough room, you might like to raise chickens and sell eggs, or grow fruit and vegetables for sale. Some people raise a specialty like mushrooms, avocados, or strawberries.

Some women learn to cut hair, or they take in washing and ironing. Others like to mind children for working mothers.

If you like photography, this makes a fine hobby and you can enter your best work in competitions, and perhaps do some semi-professional work at weddings, etc., or photograph children.

There are many women with an interest in creative writing. You can take courses in journalism, short story writing, novel writing, and even writing for TV and radio (but you must be good for that!). There are courses in Christian journalism, too. If you like writing for children, try writing first for your own youngsters and their friends, and move on to attempting to sell them to secular publishers or to those who publish Sunday school materials and the like. There are many Christian publishers in the United States. In Australia, one good secular market is the various State School magazines. They are always looking for good stories. Before you attempt to write for any publication, read the kinds of material they publish, and write for their hints to contributors, so you will know what they want. You need real talent to get far in writing, and you need perseverance as well. But many quite ordinary women can earn extra income with letters to women's magazines that pay for these, or by sending in snippets, true-life jokes, etc., to popular magazines. Greeting card companies, too, are always looking for people who can write verses, original greetings, and joke ideas for their huge supply of cards for all occasions!

Of course, if you have training for some occupation, your chances of employment will be better. If not, perhaps you can still train for some occupation that really interests you. Many mothers return to study as their children get a little older. So much training, too, can be done evenings, part time during the day, or by correspondence. But to succeed you must be serious about the work and allow yourself sufficient time to study.

If you have studied music, perhaps you are good enough, or could become good enough, to take a few students in your home. If you studied some other subject, you could possibly give coaching and private tutoring to students struggling with that subject in school.

Avenues of Service

Quite apart from ways of earning money, there are many ways the Christian woman can bless and help others. The spiritual gifts and natural talents God gives us are meant to be used. It is wrong to waste them, but it is also wrong to take on so much that we wear ourselves out. We need to focus our gifts and interests the way we focus a picture with our camera. We cannot get every part of a beautiful landscape or an interesting scene into our frame, so we select those parts most essential to a good picture. In the same way, we cannot do all the things we would like to in the church and community, so we select those things that will achieve the most and best fit our gifts. It is better to do one or two things well than half a dozen poorly!

Could you help in your church as a Sunday school teacher, a youth worker, a hospital visitor, or a women's worker? Could you lead Bible study groups or outreach groups? Could you become a lay preacher? Could you help in practical ways—bringing flowers, doing duplicating, cleaning, cooking, and giving? Could you take your turn with the tots in the nursery?

The Beautiful Ministry of the Homemaker

Your own home can also be an avenue for service. Everyday contacts with friends, relatives and neighbors may provide the opportunity to witness in a natural manner. Your home can be used for study groups or socials and for prayer meetings perhaps. Maybe you can provide hospitality for visiting preachers, missionaries, or evangelists, or to needy people in your area. Perhaps you have a ministry in letter writing, in intercession, in praying for the sick or for those seeking the fullness of the Spirit.

You may be able to use gifts in music, art, or writing for the Lord. You may have a ministry in visiting others. Remember, if you wonder where your gifts lie or if you seem to have no opportunities to use your gifts, simply start where you are with what you have—and trust God to lead on!

Enhancing Your Home and Ministry with Knowledge of the Word

Spirit-filled women will naturally wish to build up their knowledge of God's Word and of related matters as much as possible. Such knowledge will help them in their ministries and in their personal growth, and it will also make an impact on their homes and families. This knowledge is built up partly through the regular worship and ministries of the local assembly. But often we want something more systematic than this as well. Personal daily Bible study is a big help. Attending good conferences also helps, and every Christian should be a keen reader of good Christian books and magazines. When you have some good books, lend them to others, or ask if you can review the book you read in a church publication, so others may be inspired to read it. This way you will spread your blessing.

Regular Bible study groups often wander rather aimlessly. It is better to follow a plan of study through on particular subjects. Some are fortunate enough, as I and my husband have been, to attend a Bible school. Others can attend short crash courses. Evening schools and correspondence courses are helpful, because they do not interfere with our ordinary work and income.

It is worth noting one interesting new development of the last decade or two: theological or Bible education by extension, known as "Ex-Ed" or "TEE." Don't be afraid of the word "theological." It just means *serious* study of God's Word in some depth. Theological Education by Extension was first developed amid the rapidly-growing churches of Latin America, and has spread now to all the other continents and to numerous denominations, including a number of full gospel churches. These courses are available at all education levels, from beginning reader to university level, and in many languages. Each mission or denomination prepares its own courses, but often these are shared.

TEE is different from both evening college and correspondence courses, though it combines elements of both. It brings the teacher to the student, instead of vice versa. Students do most of their study at home in their own time from specially prepared books, using modern educational methods, and then attend classes in their own area every week or every two weeks with the visiting teacher. The teacher does not give a lecture, but leads a discussion and helps students develop and apply what they have studied at home. Enrichment work is also done. Thousands of students now prepare to be pastors in this way; others prepare for other ministries in the Body of Christ. Bible and practical subjects are taught, and many are finding the method a real blessing.

In some countries, many older family members do the TEE courses together. This enriches family life and conversation. If your church is interested in such a scheme for serious study of the Word and of Bible school subjects, you can obtain further information by writing to our friend Miss P. Harrison, World Evangelical Fellowship, 11 Garibaldi St., Armidale, N.S.W. 2350, Australia. She could put you in touch with others on your continent interested in TEE.

Avenues of Service for Older Women

Before we complete this section on the home, we should say a word to older women, and at the same time to younger women who because of poor health or a handicap are more than usually confined to the home. There is much these women can do to enhance the joy and love of their homes. Many of the above suggestions will apply to you also. But if you are not as active as you once were, you will still have ample opportunity to find interesting things to do and ways to bless others. Your own attitude is the key.

Be sure to remember that you are never too old to learn

more of the things of God. Giving yourself to the study of His Word will bring rich blessings. Whatever your physical limitations, you will be able to have a ministry of prayer—and there is no greater! In interceding for others, you can cover your family and relatives, your friends, and the activities of your church. You can cover your community, follow an evangelist around the country in his campaigns, or support those who pray for the sick, work as chaplains in the army, or minister in the jails. You can go to the ends of the earth with missionaries of the gospel, and all without leaving your sitting room!

To pray effectively, you need enough information. Get one or two missionary magazines regularly if possible, and support these works thoroughly. That is better than trying to pray for everything in a vague, general way. Become a prayer warrior at home and in prayer meetings for those causes which God really lays on your heart. Invite several friends to come to your home and pray with you regularly. No one knows how much has been achieved through the prayers of faithful praying women. One good idea is to "adopt" one or two missionaries or evangelists and become their special prayer partner. They will appreciate this so much. Or you may like to take the daily paper or newscast as the starting point for some prayer times; we live in a world of such need! Remember to keep a prayer diary. Then you will never lack wonderful testimonies to share with others in meetings or in person, and your heart will be full of praise for God's wonderful blessings. Those who give themselves unselfishly and seriously to prayer are at the living heart of

The Beautiful Ministry of the Homemaker

Christ's Church, close to Him. What more wonderful ministry than this?

Many older people are still quite active. If they are retired, they usually have modest but independent means, and so are able to give more time to the Lord's work than those who are still working. A husband-wife team of mature years can have a rich ministry. You have proven God over many years, and you have a wealth of experience to draw upon. It is good to share all this with the younger ones for Christ's sake. You may be able to help in counseling others, or in leading Bible classes or prayer groups. But be sure you do not live in the past. The past is to serve the present, not dominate it. You can always keep up to date, while still cherishing old values and early memories.

You need hobbies and interests, too. Many women seem to fall apart when their children leave home, yet every woman should expect this time to come and prepare for it. If we build our entire lives around our children and have no lives of our own, then this time will be much harder to face. In the same way, husbands need to prepare for retirement, and good wives can help in this. It is frightening how many men die soon after they retire; it is as if they have lost the will to live because they think their lives no longer have direction and purpose. There is no need for Christians to feel this way. There is still so much to do for the Lord and so much of His world to enjoy. Wives and husbands need to prepare together for their later years, financially but also spiritually and mentally. The time to develop hobbies and interests is when you are younger. It is very difficult to suddenly take up new interests on retirement. But if necessary, it can be done. Wives not only need to prepare for the time when their children will leave home but also for the possibility that their husbands will go to meet the Lord before they do.

One of the joys of the older woman is being a granny, perhaps even a great grandmother. You can enjoy the children without having all the responsibility of caring for them. But it is important not to spoil them, and not to interfere with their parents' way of bringing them up. Many children's lives have been richly blessed by the prayers of a devoted grandma.

Some older women are a blessing to all around them. One grandmother in her seventies recently won a "Citizen of the Year" award in her Australian country town, and it was well deserved. There are many like her. Although she had a very hard life, lost her husband when her children were young, had an operation for cancer, and brought up a family on a very small income, this woman is full of Christian joy and far too busy to feel sorry for herself. Her joy helps to keep her healthy; I am sure she will live to a ripe old age. Another older lady is always visiting lonely neighbors and shut-ins, bringing them flowers, a cake, or a word of encouragement from the Lord. She teaches a young man who had brain injuries in an accident to read again. She works tirelessly for her church. She helps run courses for Sunday school teachers and makes and sells lovely embroidery and dried-flower arrangements. She sews for busy young mothers and

The Beautiful Ministry of the Homemaker

attends Bible studies and a charismatic prayer group. She keeps a nice small garden, and she saved enough for a trip to New Zealand with a friend her own age. She writes articles for Christian women's magazines, and writes up her memories of the early days for the State School magazine. She coordinates a statewide chain of praying women.

You say, I couldn't do all those things. Perhaps not, but what *could* you do? How is your health? What are your talents and gifts? What burdens do you have? You too can radiate joy and blessing all around you—rivers of living water can flow from you if you will just let God work through you.

One retired couple in Nevada bought a camper and spent the hot desert summers visiting their relatives and touring the cooler parts of the country. They contented themselves with a smaller house so they could afford the camper, and what pleasure it brought them! They love God's natural creation. They are "rock hounds," too, and love to go out looking for interesting gemstones. Then they make their own jewelry from these. It is an interesting hobby, provides nice Christmas gifts for the family, and gives them lots of fresh air and sunshine. They have toured Alaska, Mexico, and the national parks, and they saved enough for one overseas cruise in the Pacific. Both are active in church work, too. Another retired couple worked for two years with a mission to the American Indians and loved it.

Retired couples or single folk can often make a valuable contribution to overseas missions, too, as short-termers. They are able to support themselves and, provided their doctor approves it and their health is good, they can have an interesting time serving the Lord for a year, six months, or several years in this way. There are many mission stations with good climates; many jobs are not too strenuous and do not require you to live in primitive conditions. In fact, on many mission fields today, you can live in as much comfort as at home, and this may be important if you are older. For the single or widowed older person, short-term service abroad can be wonderful—it enables you to be part of a warm Christian "family" while serving the Lord.

Some older folk serve as secretaries, as librarians for Bible schools, as houseparents in missionary children's schools, and in many other ways. If you or your husband have a profession or trade, this can generally be put to good use for the Lord. There are many necessary but unskilled jobs, too, in which you can help the missionaries. Usually, for a short-termer, it is not necessary to learn the language—you can work and live among missionaries from your own country. You can help in printing perhaps, in tape making or duplicating, in book binding or sewing, in art work or music, in running a Girls' Brigade, or in helping nurses or teachers. Such experiences can add a whole new dimension to your life. If the idea appeals to you, talk to your pastor or contact a mission board, telling them your ideas and talents.

Some older folk are even more ambitious. Grandmothers have gone to Bible school and then moved out as missionaries. One granny did this; she also studied with

The Beautiful Ministry of the Homemaker

the Summer Institute of Linguistics and then went out to help in Bible translation in a hot, remote area.

It is sad sometimes to see older Christian women sitting about doing nothing for the Lord. There is always prayer, giving, hospitality, letter writing, and visiting, at the least. Those who do nothing for the Lord often do nothing much either to cultivate their own personalities. Some sit around feeling sorry for themselves and dwelling on their half-imagined illnesses. Such people are pathetic. They have given up real living. On the other hand, it is inspiring sometimes to see how really ill and handicapped people still manage to be cheerful and even to do something to bless others. Which will be your choice?

I have written at some length about the ministries related to the home and community. This is because the home, and outreach from the home, is such a central sphere of ministry for most women. I believe firmly in family and home life, despite the efforts of some today to undermine it. Our nation will only be as strong as our homes and as the ministries we exercise in and from our homes.

PART SEVEN

Our Legal Rights in Christ

1
"Now" Power

As we draw near the end of our study, let us look a little more closely at what Christ has done for us.

Since Christ has redeemed us, women and men are *at least* back on the same level as the first man and woman before the Fall. God the Father sent His only Son, born of a woman, to make a New Contract with humankind, canceling the Old Contract (Col. 2:9-15). This Old Contract was brought in because of the Fall, and included the punishment of curses for sin. Man, woman, and all of creation suffered from the curse (Gen. 3:15-19; 2:17).

Satan's power was also broken (Col. 2:15), and the New Contract legally reconciled all things back to Christ (Col. 1:20). Christ, as the Head of the Church, has raised us up to be seated with Him, to share in reconciliation and in the authority and power of the New Contract (Eph. 1:18-23; 2:6). This means we share in Christ's own authority over all creation, and over all satanic powers!

The miracle of it all is that this reconciliation in which

we share, this liberation from the curse, this authority, is *now*. Yes, now! We are free. This is a wonderful revelation truth. Now we can use our legal rights with Christ. We realize that the complete outworking of this new freedom will await the return of Christ and the fullness of His Kingdom. That is why we still see sin and suffering on earth, and why Satan seems to have a certain power, with many still living under the curse. But the point is that *legally* that freedom and authority is ours *now*. The Kingdom of God begins at Calvary and moves on into its fullness in the coming glory. But we can enter into freedom, power, and authority now, as believers. Satan may still be roaring, for he is not yet in the bottomless pit. But he is legally bound and defeated. He cannot win; he has already lost!

You and I may claim our freedom and authority in Christ. Some of our inheritance we have already claimed, such as our salvation and the fullness of the Holy Spirit. But there is so much more. The treasure chests of our inheritance are bottomless! Some more of our inheritance can be claimed now, and we can go on drawing on His riches throughout life. Some of that inheritance we will only claim fully at the revelation of Jesus.

Hebrews 2:8 speaks of the complete reconciliation of all things to Christ. It gives us the outworking of this through faith, "Thou hast put all things in subjection under His feet." This is the New Contract in which we share. All has been put in subjection under His feet. It is legally His—and through Him, ours! Nothing was left outside Christ's authority. There may still be some skirmishes in the back provinces, but the nation, as it were, has been won. The war is over. Christ is simply awaiting the fullness of time to return and claim all that is rightfully His. He wants as many people as possible to come to salvation first.

Christ's work is legally complete. Everything is redeemed. The purchase price has been paid for every sinner to come to Him, but many still refuse His pardon. They cannot enjoy the inheritance if they will not enter into it. We cannot enjoy a generous gift of money paid into our bank accounts unless we are willing to sign and present the withdrawal slip! In the same way, you and I cannot enter into the deeper riches of our inheritance unless we "sign the withdrawal slip" with the prayer of faith or the word of faith and receive what Christ has done for us. His liberty, His authority, His riches are all there for us to draw upon.

An old Persian proverb says,

Ye dwell beside a countless store
Yet perish hungry at the door!

Is that you, dear sister, today? Enter into your inheritance! True, there are those who try to stop us from entering in. Sometimes these legalists "foes" are those of our own household, or of the household of faith. They may include some of our closest friends, some of our best-loved preachers, or the pastor of our church. Unfortunately, there are many well-meaning people around ready to tell us that "women must not do this and women must not do that."

They can usually make the reasons sound very convincing, too. They can even make it sound wonderful and feminine and godly to remain in bondage! This is the "yo-yo" problem we mentioned earlier. These people tell us how marriages have been "healed" and problems have all been solved when women gave up their inheritance and submitted (they mean "submitted" in a very different sense to the way we explained it) and when men became the "heads" (they mean "boss"—loving, but a ruler and director of the woman's whole body and soul; as we saw, this is *not* the biblical meaning). They will tell you how women found peace when they gave up their ministries. It all sounds so specious. There are always testimonies like this around to draw you away from freedom. They are called testimonies of freedom, but they are testimonies of bondage. Beware, lest you become entangled again in the yoke of bondage. Once we go back into bondage, it is always harder to come out again.

This is the trial of your faith. People will try to persuade you the message we have brought to you is extreme. They will try to water it down, agreeing with you some of the way but insisting that your freedom can only go as far as they say. They insist, too, that what they say is what the Bible says. They will give you so much freedom, like a dog on the end of a rope, while Jesus is waiting to remove the rope! For many of our readers, I believe, our message will fall on shallow, thorny ground. The seeds of liberty will spring up and flourish joyfully for a time but will soon be choked by weeds. The message has not gone deeply enough. The roots have not taken hold until that woman

"Now" Power

is quietly, lovingly unshakeable in her conviction. As a result, she will accept in the end a diluted form of the message, which seems to give her more freedom but in fact leaves her situation unchanged. Gradually the wonder of it all will fade away for women like this. They will fall back into old patterns of bondage and not emerge again. Sad to say, this is likely to happen! The same kind of thing happens with some new believers, who walk shakily with the Lord a little while and then revert to bondage. It happens, too, to many who come into the fullness of the Spirit, but are dissuaded from going on by well-meaning, sincere Christians, including "dear old Pastor So-and-So, whose wisdom I have always trusted." They do not see that even he may have a blind spot! It happens to many who receive and then lose the "new creation" message.

But we do not have to go under! We can fight our battle and win the victory of liberty, by faith. This does not mean that we tear down others, or push our views upon them prematurely. It must *never* mean that we try to *force* our husbands to see our way, or treat anyone unlovingly. Patience must be mixed with faith to inherit the promises! We may have to wait quietly until God opens the door to us. But we will not turn back or give up, or compromise our faith in freedom. We will hold on! This is a march of faith with many trials and testing before us. We are to possess the valleys and then the high mountain peaks, moving on from faith to faith, in our new-found liberty!

2
A Personal Testimony

I have told you earlier in this book a little about how God led me into wider spheres of ministry. As a woman, I have suffered deep heartache and many tears behind closed doors because of the overwhelming feelings of rejection and inferiority which filled me. No one will ever know the sufferings these caused me.

Furthermore, I was taught that as a woman I was not worth nearly as much as a man. This was the implication of many messages I heard. Women, I soon came to realize, were second-rate citizens. Our main purpose in living was apparently to look after our menfolk and bear children. As the Germans used to say, woman's role was centered around just three things—*Kinder, Kirche, Küche*—children, church, and kitchen!

I had no self-confidence at all. I wanted to be seen and not heard, to retire timidly and remain in the background. I would never have imagined that one day I would be brave enough to stand up and address great crowds of people with God's message! I wondered why God made women to be so inferior, why He didn't seem to like us much or want us to do anything.

Yet all through this time, the calling of God was on my life. I could not understand it and often pleaded with God to release me from it. But God's callings are strong and sure, and He would not remove it.

Through heartache and heartbreak, He led me on to higher ground. He compelled me with His own compassion and sweetness to "get off the briar and get on the wing" (like the mother eagle compelling her little eaglets to leave the nest and learn to fly—Deut. 32:11-12). My ministry and leadership gifts prompted me from within my very nature. These gifts were actually part of my makeup, but had been crushed and broken by the legalistic teachings of those who believe that for women there is no redemption from the curse. Satan also deluded me in this way, for he has hated woman from the beginning (Gen. 3:14-15).

Gradually, the gift made a way for itself under God's hand. Inferiorities were broken off me and confidence imparted. As the old hymn puts it:

Down in the human heart
Crushed by the Tempter,
Feelings lie buried, that grace can restore.

Touched by a loving hand,
Wakened by kindness,
Chords that were broken will vibrate once more!
    (Verse 3 of "Rescue the Perishing"
      by Frances Jane van Alstyne)

A Personal Testimony

As I explained earlier, in time I was given governmental responsibility as pastor of a substantially-sized church with several outreach centers. The fruits of my pastoral ministry were manifested not only in the assembly, but also in the school of evangelism we started to train men and women for ministry all over Australia. My husband and I had raised up churches. We had ministered to them, and now they were also ministering to us. Our charismatic organization had put their seal of recognition upon the ministry. God called my husband then to move out to other cities to pioneer more charismatic centers. For a time, our ministries progressed separately to an extent, as he had to be away, and I had the church to take care of. Occasionally I traveled with him. Sometimes we have to make sacrifices like this in our ministry. We were still a team, but his work at that time was church planting, while mine was pastoring the newly formed church. We appreciated each other all the more at those times when we could be together. I pastored for five years. Then God called us both further afield. We became landed immigrants in Canada, and lived there for a few years. This became our home base, and from there we moved out to ministry in the United States and in other lands. We conducted large crusades in India every year. Later we returned to Australia as our headquarters to set up our worldwide ministry. Like all ministers, I exercise my authority under His authority. I work under the headship of Christ, while seated with Him in heavenly places and sharing in His inheritance and power (Eph. 2:10).

Many churches have only very recently begun to accept

WOMEN IN MINISTRY TODAY

women ministers. We see it as part of the same restoration of genuine Christianity which began in the Reformation and is now being evidenced in the charismatic movement. Little by little over the years, God is lifting His people back out of the darkness of unregenerate religion, out of unbiblical teachings and practices. We learn slowly, but do we learn!

We know that there were many women ministering in various ways in the New Testament Church. In the first century there were evidently a lot more, including women apostles, preachers and so on. But Church history shows us that in the second century churchmen made a concerted effort to remove women from positions of authority and ministry. And since then, women—half the human race—have been very largely excluded from any real authority or ministry. Many have had unofficial ministries of great power, nonetheless, and many of the nuns of the Middle Ages also exercised powerful ministries, even though the Church would not allow them to be priests. At the Reformation, Luther reaffirmed the great principle of the priesthood of all believers, so clearly taught in Scripture, but he did not understand that this was meant to include women! Luther, like some of the other Reformers, had a low view of women. Thus, for several hundred years, people have talked about the priesthood of all believers, when they mean, in fact, the priesthood of only half the believers (less than half really, as there are more Christian women than men).

In reality, even the priesthood of all men was not carried out very fully. Church services were still largely di-

A Personal Testimony

rected by one man, and we do not find very much evidence of real team ministry and of wide exercise of the gifts until the time of the pentecostal revivals.

As the real meaning of priesthood began to be understood, a few women have had real ministries in charismatic and other churches. Some of the founders of the pentecostal movement were women with remarkable ministries. But in general, most of the time, all the speakers at charismatic conventions were men. All those in authority were men. The same was generally true in charismatic churches. We found very few women ministers in our midst. But there has been a change in the last two years. Women ministers have increased, and women have increased as charismatic convention speakers.

Actually, God opened the way for me to be ordained nearly a decade ago in our denomination. We are a charismatic fellowship, only twenty years old, but born in revival and open to God. Our church has a good, enlightened policy on women's ministries, recognizing there is still room for many more women to exercise ministry gifts in our midst. Some of our churches are very large by Australian pentecostal standards; others are smaller but thriving assemblies.

Because of my ordination, I have gained recognition from other mainline and pentecostal organizations in Australia and in several countries. Some Christian papers and magazines have printed my story. Our denomination bestowed a great honor on me, for I did not apply for ordination. However, I was pastoring a good-sized church in practice, though without official papers, at the time ordination was suggested. The gift made way for itself, and they recognized the fruit of the ministry. I was the first woman pastor, and there are no others as yet. But the doors are open. In addition, a number of our women do hold special credentials as missionaries on the mission fields.

Although God has enabled me to do the work of a pastor, I do not believe this is my special gift. God has given me another related gift, which I will not discuss here. However, our gifts often overlap with others, and it is sometimes difficult to define exactly what our gifts or talents are. Never mind then, if you are not quite sure what yours is. If you know the kind of ministry you fulfill successfully, then that is the way to go! There are a number of gifts mentioned in Scripture, far more than usually listed, and there are probably others, as well, not specifically mentioned in Scripture. Every gift is important, so none of my readers should feel bad if they do not feel called as I was to a preaching or pastoring ministry. It is not for everyone. *Whatever* your gift is, God wants to bless it and use it. It need not be a very public one. Move out now and receive His good gifts to you! Be what He wants you to be, and do what He wants you to do.

In Closing: From the Heart of the Author

The most *joyous* thing I know is deliverance from the bondages of all the principles of law into the glorious liberty in Christ Jesus. To be set free is like a bird let out of a cage to fly away to its own resting place. But the most *glorious* thing I know is to find this resting place in the *agape* love. As this death to legalism and self is actively at work in us, a new kind of life is released to all our loved ones. We are freed from our self to a spirit of giving (2 Cor. 4:12, TAB).

When the Lord sets us free and places us in the pathway of walking in the Spirit, in His depth, He also commissions us to "go ye into all the world and preach the gospel" in the power and love we have received in Him. We are to share the goodness and grace of our Lord Jesus Christ with others, not withholding His grace. Poised in spirit, we should be always ready to shine, always ready to give to the poor, always ready to support the mission fields.

There is a special anointing upon the support of mission work, because it is the unselfishness of God's heart working through us to the underprivileged nations of the world. Mission work is a vision that goes beyond our own privileged nation, beyond ourselves. Giving is the heart of God.

Bibliography

Reference Books:
The following books were used in this study:
Bauer (trs. Arndt and Gingrich). *A Greek-English Lexicon of the New Testament.* Chicago: University of Chicago Press, 1969.
Brown, Driver and Briggs (Gesenius). *A Hebrew and English Lexicon of the Old Testament.* Oxford: Clarendon Press, 1966.
Dake, Finis J. *Annotated Reference Bible: The New Testament.* Grand Rapids: Zondervan, 1961.
Hendriksen, William. *Ephesians.* Banner of Truth Trust, 1967.
Young, R. *Analytical Concordance to the Bible.* Grand Rapids: Eerdmans, 1970.
Also consulted were numerous English versions of the Bible, and several other standard commentaries, concordances, word studies, Bible handbooks and books on Bible times and customs.

Resources on the Ministry of Women:
In this book, we have only introduced the reader to some of the biblical interpretation which has been done in this subject area. Those who wish to do more detailed study on the roles and ministries of women from the biblical standpoint are advised to consult some of the following books. Most are readily available through Christian

bookstores and can be ordered if not in stock. A few are out of print and would only be found in libraries, etc., and one or two are unpublished. They represent several viewpoints.

Boldrey, Richard and Joyce. *Chauvinist or Feminist? Paul's View of Women*. Grand Rapids: Baker Book House, 1976. This book contains a very useful booklist for further reading.

Booth, Catherine. *Female Ministry: Woman's Right to Preach the Gospel*. London: 1859; New York: Salavation Army, 1975. Over 100 years ago, the Salvation Army recognized the right of women to preach the Word. They led the world in this recognition and wrote into their basic laws a clause forbidding anyone to hinder women from holding office in the Salvation Army, or to prevent them from preaching or voting. In this book, the saintly Catherine Booth explains the biblical reasons for this pioneering stand for liberty.

Bushnell, Katherine. *God's Word to Women*. Order from Mr. Ray Munson, Box 52, N. Collins, New York 14111, U.S.A.

Chaney, Thelma. *The Ministry of Women in the Church*. Charismatic. Order from 636 E. Third St., Tulsa, Oklahoma 74120, U.S.A.

Daley, Mary. *The Church and the Second Sex*. New York: Harper and Row, 1975. A modern Catholic perspective.

Giles, Kevin. *The Ministry of Women: A New Look at an Old Question*. Melbourne: Dove Publications, in press. By an Anglican minister.

Harper, Joyce. *Women and the Gospel*. A Christian Brethren Research Fellowship Occasional Paper. 34 Tekesbury Ave., Pinner, Middlesex, England.

Harrison, Patricia. Several unpublished papers on the exegesis of passages concerning women.

Harrison, J. Pearson. *Should Women Preach?* Pamphlet, out of print. A clear, concise affirmation of women's ministry by a famous Australian Baptist minister of some years ago.

Jewett, Paul K. *Man as Male and Female*. Grand Rapids: Eerdmans, 1975. A detailed study by a well-known and highly-trained professor of evangelical theology.

Bibliography

Mollenkott, Virginia Ramey. *Women, Men and the Bible.* Nashville: Abingdon, 1977. An excellent short book describing the Christian way of human relationships, "mutual submission."

Morris, Leon, Gaden, John, and Thiering, Barbara. *A Woman's Place.* Sydney, 1976. Anglican Doctrine Commission Papers on the role of women in the Church.

Penn-Lewis, Jessie. *Magna Carta of Women.* Publisher unknown, out of print. The deeply spiritual woman who played so big a role in the Welsh revivals shares in this book the revelation God gave her concerning the freedom of women.

Porter, Sue Ellen. California, 1967 and 1968. Several unpublished papers on the detailed exegesis of Bible passages.

Scanzoni, L., and Hardest, N. *All We're Meant To Be: A Biblical Approach to Women's Liberation.* Waco, Texas: Word Books, 1975.

Starr, Lee Anna. *The Bible Status of Women.* Old Tappan, N.J.: Fleming H. Revell, 1926. Out of print, but the publisher is considering a reprint. This is the most comprehensive study of the subject probably to have appeared anywhere, by a very learned woman with two doctoral degrees and a profound knowledge of Scripture and its original languages.

Thiering, Barbara. *Created Second?* Family Life Movement of Australia, 1973.

Tiemeyer, Raymond, ed. *The Ordination of Women.* Minneapolis: Augsburg Publishing House, 1970. Report authorized by the Division of Theological Studies of the Lutheran council in the U.S.A.

Other Books Worth Reading

Beaver, R. Pierce. *All Loves Excelling.* Grand Rapids: Eerdmans, 1968.

Craft, Ruth. *Play School Play Ideas.* London, BBC, 1971. Lots of ideas for mothers with young children who want them to learn to make and do things. From BBC's "Play School." Also available from ABC offices, Australia.

Dobson, James. *Dare to Discipline.* Wheaton, Ill.: Tyndale, 1971. A Christian psychologist offers sensible advice to parents and teachers. Also available with a cassette and study guide for groups.

Flexner, Eleanor. *Century of Struggle: The Women's Rights Movement in the U.S.* Cambridge: Harvard University Press, and New York: Atheneum, 1968. Traces the hardy pioneers from the Mayflower to the vote which was won in 1920. A moving history. Various other women's histories are available.

Dixson, Miriam. *The Real Matilda: Women and Identity in Australia 1788 to 1975.* New York: Penguin Books, 1976. Another history of women. The author has done a serious study and finds the Australian past steeped in negative feelings about women.

Friedan, Betty. *The Feminine Mystique.* New York: Dell Publishing Co., 1977. An absorbing, thoroughly documented study. Well worth having.

Gavron, Hannah. *The Captive Wife: Conflicts of Housebound Mothers.* New York: Penguin Books, 1966. A perceptive study of some common problems.

Hunt, Gladys. *Honey for a Child's Heart: The Imaginative Use of Books in Family Life.* Grand Rapids: Zondervan, 1975. A delightful book for Christian parents. There are several good books available on children's literature. Another good one is Lillian Smith's *The Unreluctant Years: A Critical Approach to Children's Literature* (New York: Viking Press, 1967). This book is not specifically Christian, but is very worthwhile. To give your child an appetite for fine books and literature, Christian and general, is one of the most precious gifts you can pass on.

Ibsen, Henrik. *A Doll's House.* A classic play by the great Norwegian dramatist, written first in 1879, available now in many English editions and in movie form. One edition containing this famous play is the Penguin Classics edition of Ibsen's plays. The play tells

Bibliography

(before its time really) a lot about women and freedom. Another play of Ibsen's on the same subject, *The Lady From the Sea,* is also included in the Penguin edition.

Macksey, Joan and Kenneth. *The Guinness Guide to Feminine Achievements.* Enfield, England: Guinness Superlatives, Ltd., 1975. 2 Cecil Court, London Road, Enfield, Middlesex, England.

Narramore, Bruce. *Help! I'm a Parent.* Grand Rapids: Zondervan, 1972. A biblical and psychological approach to child rearing. A manual accompanies this for use in small groups if desired. The manual, called *A Guide to Child Rearing,* contains many practical exercises for parents.

Price, Eugenia. *Woman to Woman.* Grand Rapids: Zondervan, 1960. A woman well known for her ministry all over America, whose books have sold many thousands of copies, tells us the meaning of a Christ-controlled personality. She is single, and although she speaks also to wives and mothers, she has something special for single girls as well. See also her book, *Share My Precious Stones.*

Rapoport, Rhona and Robert. *Dual-Career Families.* New York: Penguin Books, 1971. A highly competent husband-wife team of sociologists have compiled a careful study on the joys and problems of the family where both parents work. This is a government survey from Britain.

Schaeffer, Edith. *Hidden Art.* England: Norfolk Press, 1972. A delightful book (makes a fine gift too) for homemakers by the wife of the well-known Christian writer, Francis Schaeffer. She shows how we can find art and beauty hidden in the everyday things, and how we can bring beauty and joy into our homes in dozens of ways. Lots of practical suggestions for the home and for working with our children. Christian perspective throughout.

ten Boom, Corrie. *The Hiding Place.* Old Tappan, N.J.: Fleming H. Revell (Spire), 1974. A wonderfully inspiring true story by a brave, Spirit-filled Dutch woman. Read her other books, too, and look for further books about the ministries of Christian women. These will encourage you.

WOMEN IN MINISTRY TODAY

Some of these books are Christian, and some are not. They represent many different viewpoints. Most are either paperbacks or moderately priced. Their views do not necessarily represent those of the author of this book. There are a great number of books which can help you be a fuller person, a better wife and mother, and one who can handle new freedom and responsibility in a Christlike way. Look for them in your bookstores and share them with your friends. Remember, however, that most books on the family sold in Christian bookstores today follow the traditional, not-very-free view of women. They have much good material in them, but they fail to recognize woman's real freedom in Christ.